DATE DUE			

HIGHSMITH #45114

The Exotic Kitchens of
MALAYSIA

The Exotic Kitchens of
MALAYSIA

COPELAND MARKS

DONALD I. FINE BOOKS

DONALD I. FINE BOOKS
Published by the Penguin Group
Penguin Putnam Inc., 375 Hudson Street,
New York, New York 10014, U.S.A.
Penguin Books Ltd, 27 Wrights Lane,
London W8 5TZ, England
Penguin Books Australia Ltd, Ringwood,
Victoria, Australia
Penguin Books Canada Ltd, 10 Alcorn Avenue,
Toronto, Ontario, Canada M4V 3B2
Penguin Books (N.Z.) Ltd, 182–190 Wairau Road,
Auckland 10, New Zealand

Penguin Books Ltd, Registered Offices:
Harmondsworth, Middlesex, England

First published by Donald I. Fine Books,
an imprint of Penguin Putnam Inc.

First Printing, November, 1997
10 9 8 7 6 5 4 3 2 1

Copyright © Copeland Marks, 1997
Map by Patricia Tobin Fein

Illustrations from the Brooklyn Botanic Garden's handbook
Oriental Herbs and Vegetables, 1983, reprinted with the permission of
Stephen K-M. Tim and the Brooklyn Botanic Garden.

LIBRARY OF CONGRESS CATALOGING IN PUBLICATION DATA

Marks, Copeland.
    The exotic kitchens of Malaysia / Copeland Marks.
        p.   cm.
    ISBN 1-55611-526-1
    1. Cookery, Malaysian.   I. Title.
TX724.5.M4M36   1997
641.59595—dc21   97-11377
                                         CIP

Printed in the United States of America
Set in 11/14 Cochin
Designed by Irving Perkins Associates, Inc.

CONTENTS

Acknowledgments

I am a culinary tourist who moves from one region of the country I am writing about to another, stopping now and then to cook and record the culinary facts of life.

I wish to thank Azizah Aziz, Vice President of the Malaysia Tourism Promotion Board, New York City, and her staff, who assisted my project to write the national cookbook of Malaysia. With enthusiasm, intelligence, and knowledge of their craft, they made my journey easy and effective.

Also, Malaysia Airlines, with its professionalism and practical advice and help, gave me great confidence in its ability to transport the world.

In the cities and *kampongs*, the wonderful people of Malaysia assisted me with cheerfulness and pride in their styles of cooking.

Kuala Lumpur
    Loke Wai Keng (Nonya)
    Annie (Daisy) Roseling
    Francis Xavier
    Chef Sam Ramasamy—preeminent in the Malaysian-Indian cooking style

Malacca
    Chef Lim Jit Hin
    Pauline Fernandes (Nonya)

Ipoh
    Chef Ramu Suppiah
    Chef Chia Kok Sing
    Chef Foo Kien Yuk (Ken)
    Zubidi Abul Ghaffar

Mohd Rafie Mohd Taib
Norbibi Manaf
Chef Jasri Abbas

PENANG
Chef Kwah Kar Khock
Lee Eng Huat

ALOR SETAR
Chef Lim Kim Sek
Chef Zakaria Hassan

KOTA BAHRU
Hajjah Nik Faizah (the Sultan's cook)
Chef Hamzah Harun
Chef Din Dolla
Khairah Ikhwan Khalil

TERENGGANU
Chef Ismail Hashim
Chef Rahimee Kassim

KUANTAN
Chef Razali B. Abd Rahman
Chef Tan Jok Bu

KOTA KINABALU, SABAH, BORNEO
Evelene Mingrong
Mansore Sulaiman

KUCHING, SARAWAK, BORNEO
Audry Wan Ullok
Empaga, the Iban
Giake, the Bidayuh
Inyau Stephen, the Iban
Batis Lakut (Kampong Padang Pan)

NEW YORK

Faridah Nadzim
Wan Badariah Sinon
Nik Rauha Kamarkudin
Saradha Thanaraja Singam
Emily Chen Sian Yin (Hakka, Ipoh)
Ipoh Garden

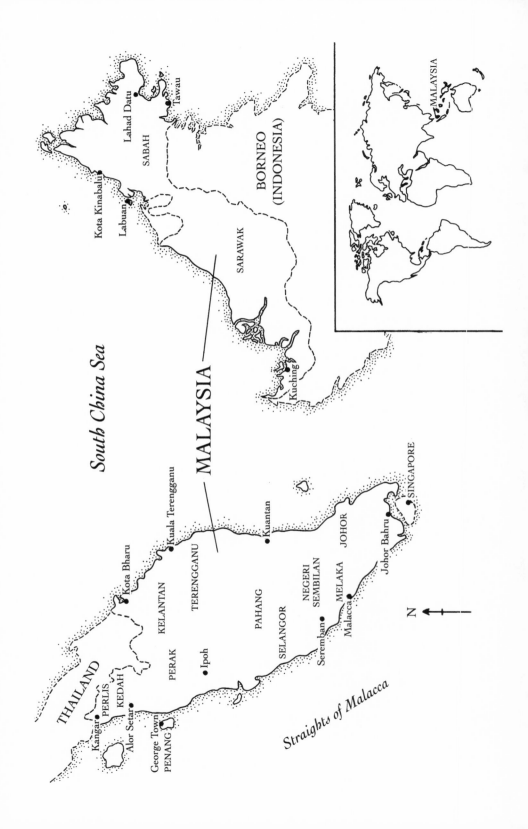

INTRODUCTION

Some years ago I lived in Singapore for a year, during the era when it was known as old Singapore, with its narrow alleys and very slow pace. Now everything has changed, with glittery twentieth-century living and a pace that is, to say the least, intense. But my mind has been on Malaysia for a long time and its unknown culinary pleasures that have been influenced by Thailand on the north and Indonesia in the south. But the drummer is Malaysian.

In 1995, I traveled to Malaysia and did research on the regional cooking styles in all of the major cities on the eastern and western sides of the peninsula. Then I went to Borneo to study the indigenous people in the two states of Sabah and Sarawak. It was a revelation: I was able to capture the fundamental style of the cooking in the shape of more than two hundred marvelous recipes!

The Country and Its People

In 1511, at the height of the colonial period, the Portuguese conquered Malacca in the southern portion of the Malay Peninsula and, in effect, started the culinary diversity of Malaysia. Later, the Dutch, in 1641, and the British, in 1815, completed the European intrusions.

Malaysia is fortunate from a culinary point of view for its great diversity of racial groups and religions and for the natural ingenuity of the people with their gastronomic preoccupation. The tropical climate there produces an overflowing cornucopia of fruits and vegetables, as well as herbs of an exotic nature not known in Europe. Thus, the dishes that developed from these fragrant and sometimes bizarre ingredients produced a world-class revolution in the origins of cuisines. Take curry, for example, and its pervasive hold on the kitchen gods of the homemaker.

The three great communities that comprise the population of Malaysia are the Malays, Chinese, and Indians. From each of these emerged a marvelous style of cooking and culinary identity. The motto "you are what you eat" was never more true than there, as it identifies the three communities, each of which has a tendency to stick to its own cooking.

In addition, to compound the diversity of the available foods, is the cooking of the indigenous people *(orang ulu)* of the two Malaysian states in Borneo—Sarawak and Sabah. Here one finds the Iban, Bidayuh, and Kadazan, some of them head hunters in earlier times, but now having moved into the twentieth century, ruined forever with less interesting pursuits. Their foods are simple and very tasty, and are currently developing more complexity. I have spent time with all these people in their *kampongs* (villages).

Malays

The Malays are the original inhabitants of the Malay Peninsula and they march to a distinct culinary drummer. They use hot chilis with generosity. Coconut milk enriches their curries that are made with shallots, ginger, garlic, galangal, and the intense *belacan* (fermented shrimp cake), which is employed sparingly but effectively.

The Malays are Muslim and do not eat pork. Most of their dishes center on beef and seafood and, on occasion, mutton (lamb).

The most popular dish found all over Malaysia and in all communities is the satay, or barbecue, grilled on short wooden skewers. Peanut sauces of many varieties are served with the barbecued meats or seafood and are essential to the overall presentation of this beloved dish.

The Chinese

No one who has spent time in Malaysia can be unaware of the sheer quantity, quality, and variety of the Chinese Malaysian cuisine. The center for all this eating, especially after seven in the evening, occurs in the essentially Chinese cities of Ipoh and on the island of Penang, although every city has a sprinkling of popular restaurants. The food is not a carbon copy of the Chinese mainland cuisine, but reflects the influences of centuries of Chinese experience on the Malay Peninsula.

The food is regional. Certain dishes are associated with cities and gourmets travel there to taste it. In Ipoh, for example, there is the well-known Nasi Ayam (Chicken Rice), which is simple in style and served with bean sprouts of a special variety not found elsewhere. In Penang, it is the phenomenon of the hawker food, food carts, hundreds of them, that are pushed into their localities with their special fast foods of seafood, poultry, rice, noodles, soups, or any other dish of family origin. Hawker food is cheap and the eating courts are filled until the late hours with families out on the town, including small children. The Chinese are an eating society.

The collection of Chinese dishes is traditional, varied, and ingenious, with the flavors of shallots, ginger, garlic, and discreetly fresh chilis but without the volume of spices that the Malays and Indians use.

The Indians

The Indians, who are a small percentage of the population in Malayasia, immigrated from south India, and their food reflects their origin. There are Hindu and Muslim Indians, and each has a separate style of cooking. The Hindus do not eat beef; the Muslims do not eat pork. Both groups use a catalogue of spices and seasonings, with, perhaps, the edge for using chilis going to the Muslim community.

Of special interest are the banana-leaf restaurants that are thronged with diners during the lunch hour. The dishes consist of generous quantities of rice, with the choice of vegetarian curries or meat and fish dishes, all served on a banana leaf—no plates!

The Muslim menu is rich with spices, meat, and seafood. The hot chili sometimes reigns supreme. Rice tempers the intensity of the chili. Roti Canai (Crisp Fried Pancakes, page 24) are universally popular and justifiably so.

Indian food can be characterized as cheap, spicy, full of flavor, and lacking the subtleties of Chinese cooking. Malaysians of every community like the Indian food.

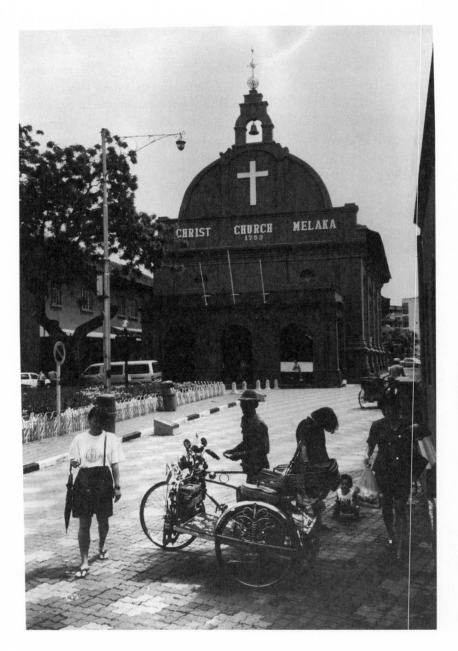

Early Portuguese colonial church, Malacca.

Nonya

The small community of Nonya is crosscultural, Chinese men who during the colonial period married Malay women. They are known as Straits-born Chinese of Malacca. Their food is a combination of Chinese/Malay and has developed its own style and intensity. It is distinctive, and there are those who dote on its idiosyncrasies of powerful curries and spicy side dishes. The Nonyas of Malacca and Penang, the two regions where they originated, have shades of differences in the flavors of the foods they prepare.

Portuguese

There are vestiges of the Portuguese conquest of 1511. Their ancestors are the Eurasians of Malacca and they, too, have foods associated with the colonial experience, which are sometimes equated with the Nonya.

The Indigenous Peoples of Borneo

The northern third of Borneo has two Malaysian states, Sabah, which is in the east, and Sarawak in the west. They are another world, almost totally detached from mainland Malaysia. The southern part of Borneo is called Kalimantan and is a possession of Indonesia.

The state of Sabah has the Kadazan people and their style of cooking. Sarawak, a former British possession, has the Iban and Bidayuh tribes and their style. Both of the states have a sprinkling of Chinese, Indian Muslims, and Malays and eating houses, where one can sample the always excellent food.

Neither group of indigenous people has restaurants, so one goes into the interior or arranges with an ethnic friend to cook for a traditional meal in the city. I did both. The food is simple, with recognizable ingredients. Living off the land is paramount to their cooking. The fresh fruit, vegetables, and the poultry that runs around the *kampong*, eating clean, unpolluted greens, make all the difference. Recipes of this honest home cooking are included.

· · ·

The American reader and cook has developed a sense of adventure that was not readily apparent in the past. The insatiable search for adventure has made all my books continuous sellers. They reach the adventurous public who like to read cookbooks and cook from them.

All the ingredients that are called for in the pages that follow are available, with the exception of extreme rarities. In those cases, I offer substitutes. Asian markets in the English-speaking world are geared to the movement of Asians from one geographical location to another and their ingredients follow them into food shops.

Since I have lived and traveled in Asia for many years, my acquaintance with the cuisines there (plus my books) has made it possible for me to state assuredly that the various cuisines of Malaysia will become part of our culinary experience here. The food of Malaysia is wonderful!

HAWKER FOOD (IPOH AND PENANG)

Years ago, during my residence in Singapore, Chinese hawkers used to walk their wares through the streets. There were cooked foods, such as noodles, soups, roast duck, chicken, pork, vegetables — everything for the housekeepers who did not want to cook and at very reasonable prices. These itinerant salesmen carried their wares in two large baskets balanced over their shoulders on a sturdy bamboo pole. The hawkers announced their arrival by slapping two pieces of wood together in an identifiable rhythm — click, click, clack, or clack, clack, click, click. At the sound, you looked out the window to see who was selling what.

All that is gone now. Modernization in the form of sanitation, crowded streets, permanently situated restaurants, and city administrators has retired the classic colonial old-time ambiance. In exchange, we now have air pollution.

Hawker food is still available, relegated to small locations or found in larger food courts, often on street corners that open to the public. In one I frequented, there were nine different stalls on moveable carts arranged around the edge of the space facing the street. Tables and chairs were available.

Each cook did his or her own things, be it noodles, meats, snacks. The choice was yours, and you paid for what you got at a price so reasonable that I wondered why anyone bothered to cook at home. Lunch was a busy hour, and much later in the day, after seven in the evening, crowds appeared again, foraging for food.

The hawkers are now anchored to a permanent spot.

GLOSSARY

Asafetida *(Ferula assafoetida)* is a member of the carrot family and is known by the Indians in their curries as *hing*. It has a powerful aroma, which some people consider offensive, and is used in small quantities (about ⅛ teaspoon or less) to add dimension to the food.

Belacan *(fermented shrimp cake)* is one of the very important seasonings of Malaysian cooking. The tiny shrimp are fermented with salt, then pressed into firm cakes of about 5 ounces, depending upon the company that makes them. In addition to adding a subtle flavor to curry or other meat, fish, or vegetable combinations, *belacan* contains considerable protein.

The use of fermented shrimp or anchovy paste or essence has a common theme in Southeast Asia. The Burmese, Thais, and Vietnamese use a liquid fish sauce called, variously, *nam pya ye* or *nam pla*. The Indonesians use *trassi*, a spinoff of the same thing with a toothpaste consistency, and the Malaysians prefer *belacan*, the cake that is sliced.

Belacan must be lightly toasted for 1 to 2 minutes, until the aroma arises, in an oven or toaster oven before using.

Candlenut *(Aleurites triloba)* is known as *buah keras* in Malaysia and *kemiri* in Indonesia. When ground up, it is used as a thickener in curry sauces. It can be found in Asian groceries, but if not, macadamia nuts are a legitimate substitution.

Coconut Milk For instructions on preparing fresh coconut milk at home, see How To Make, page 286. That said, it seems that canned coconut milk imported from Thailand (Chaokoh brand) is the preferred choice of many these days. The canned milk is thick and heavy and should be diluted in most cases before using. For how I dilute it into "regular," the consistency most frequently called for in the recipes here, see page 14.

Curry Powders Malaysians use curry powder without guilt, unlike some of the purists in the United States. There are several commercial varieties, one for meat, and another for fish and seafood. The powders are fresh, potent, and available and contain traditional spices such as star anise, clove, cinnamon, and cardamom, the flavorings that typify much of the Malaysian culinary tradition.

Galangal *(Alpinia galanga)* is known as *lengkuas* in Malaysia. A botanical relative of ginger, it has a similar root-like appearance. It has a distinctive and powerful flavor, however, and is frequently used in various curries, leaving an attractive footprint. In the sixteenth century, it was praised for providing good digestion, sweet breath, and stimulation of carnal desire. Wow!

Ginger Bud *(Phaeomaria)* has the local name of *bunga kantan*. This is a beautiful pink bud, about 3 inches, long found in public markets in Malaysia and collected in the wild. Slices of the bud are added to curries, adding a ginger-like fragrance. It is available in Southeast Asian markets, that is to say Thailand, Malaysia, or so on.

Gula Malacca *(Arenga saccharifera)* is palm sugar, an extraordinary dark brown sugar produced from the sugar palm tree. The caramel flavor is rich and dense, with a sweetness that differs from cane sugar. This singular sugar is used in sweets, curries, or anywhere else in Malaysian cooking where a traditional flavor is wanted.

Ikan Bilis are dried baby anchovies, and a ubiquitous sight in the public markets. The tiny creatures are prepared in several tasty ways. They can be pan or deep fried to a light brown crisp in a very short time over low heat and used as a garnish on rice or curries. Or they can be eaten out of hand with, perhaps, a glass of wine, as I do. Or you can enjoy them in a stir-fried Sambal Goreng Nenas (page 234).

Jícama *(yam bean) (Pachyrhizus erosus)* has the local name of *bangkuang*. The first time I tasted the jícama was in Mexico, where it may have originated botanically. It looks like an overgrown potato, a flattened tuber with rounded bulges. Most of the time the white flesh is eaten fresh and with a juicy crunch as in Rojak (page 208), but it can be included in stir-fried vegetable dishes as well.

Kicip *(black soy sauce)* is a heavy, slightly sweet sauce made from molasses, salt, soy bean, and flour. *Kicip* is reminiscent of the Indonesian *kecap* but not as sweet or thick. I prefer the Koon Chun brand from Hongkong.

Lemongrass *(Cymbopogon citratus)* is known as *serai* in the local language. I have seen fields of lemongrass growing in Guatemala, but no one used it there in the cooking. Malaysia, Indonesia, Thailand, and others know what a remarkable seasoning it is in traditional foods. A subtle lemon flavor is the characteristic most noticed but with a fresh grassy aroma as well.

The root end of the lemongrass bundle has the most flavor. The inner part of the root end is soft and can be sliced or crushed in a processor. When the bundle is older and hard it can be firmly whacked with a mallet and included in the dish, where the flavor is released. Only about five or six inches above the root end on a stalk of lemongrass is used.

Pandan *(of the Pandanus species)* is known as screwpine. One of the basic elements of Malaysian cooking, the long, green leaves when crushed have a sweet, aromatic aroma and a green color used to tint foods. Plants grow everywhere and are instantly available in family gardens. Pandan juice, in particular, is used in sweets and desserts to provide its popular aroma as well as the color. If pandan leaves are unavailable, a bottled imitation pandan essence is available in some Southeast Asian markets.

Petis udang *(shrimp paste)* is a thick, black paste used in Chinese dishes. It is always purchased, and the one I have in my refrigerator was made in Penang. It is prepared from "prawn juice, sugar, flour, and salt" and is without an offensive aroma.

Tofu Skin Sticks result from the manufacture of tofu. The long dried sticks are rolled into 12-inch or longer lengths. They should be soaked in water for 1 hour, until soft and flexible, then cut to the desired length. Tofu skin sticks are an admirable ingredient in stir-fried vegetarian dishes.

Wood Ears *(Auricularia sp.)* are a large black fungus with off-white sections that give it an artistic appearance. They are easily found in Chinese groceries. Soak the fungi covered in water for 1 hour until they soften to a smooth leathery texture, then slice according to the recipe.

RICE, PANCAKES, AND NOODLES

China and India have had an enormous influence on the cuisines of Malaysia. The history of rice in Asia begins in China and later in India, so it is logical that rice has become the traditional and indispensable grain in Malaysia. Rice dominates the diet. It is served boiled plain or seasoned with meats, spices, and seasonings, when it is elevated to finer culinary heights.

Garden in Buddhist temple in Ipoh.

Long- and short-grain rices are the most common, but there is the glutinous or sticky rice that is used in making rice wine and an assortment of desserts and sweets.

As to the pancake part of it, Masala Thosai (page 19) is the Indian pancake prepared from rice and glorified in several ways. *Roti canai* is the Indian wheat pancake that may be the most popular breakfast and snack food in Malaysia. For this wonderful dish see page 24.

Noodles *(bihun)* prepared from rice flour are another popular method of presenting this grain. Rice noodles are a Chinese invention and eaten all over Malaysia.

And then there is black rice, which makes for a very tasty dessert.

NASI LEMAK (MALAY)
Rice in Coconut Milk

This could also be called breakfast rice since it is served with an assortment of sambals for breakfast. I have tasted *nasi lemak* with crispy fried baby anchovies, a chili-hot side dish (sambal) of the anchovies in a stew, roasted peanuts, and sliced cucumber, all of it sprinkled over a tempting heap of the rice. This is traditional food that sticks to the ribs.

4   *cups rice, well rinsed in cold water*
1   *cup "regular" coconut milk (see page 14)*
4   *cups water*
4   *slices of ginger, peeled*
1/4 *teaspoon salt*

> Put all the ingredients in an automatic rice cooker (a most popular method all over Malaysia) and steam until ready. Be certain to use the proportions for the rice cooker based upon the above quantities.
>
> This rice dish may also be cooked in the conventional method by bringing all the ingredients noted above to a rapid boil. Lower the heat to very low, cover the pan, and cook for 15 minutes, stirring once or twice during this time. Remove from the heat and let stand, covered, 10 minutes before serving. Or, utilize your own favorite method of cooking rice.
>
> Serve with an assortment of side dishes for breakfast or lunch.
>
> SERVES 8 OR MORE.

Nasi Dagang #1 (Malay)

Traditional Rice from Kelantan

Regional styles of cooking rice are common in Malaysia. In the eastern state of Kelantan, I enjoyed for breakfast a soft rice that was similar to what the Koreans prefer and a mild (for me) fish curry. It seemed appropriate for the ambiance.

4   *cups short-grain soft rice*
2   *cups "light" coconut milk (see Note below)*
1   *teaspoon fenugreek seed (*halba *in Malay)*
3   *shallots, sliced*
    a 1-inch piece young ginger, sliced thin
1   *teaspoon salt, or to taste*
1/2 *teaspoon sugar*

1. Soak the rice in water to cover for 1 hour. Drain. Steam the rice, covered, over boiling water for 1/2 hour and transfer it to a pan. Add the "light" coconut milk, bring to a boil, cover, and cook over low heat for 10 minutes.
2. Combine the fenugreek seeds, shallots, ginger, salt, and sugar. Add to the rice, cover, and simmer over low heat for 10 minutes.
   Serve warm.

SERVES 10 OR MORE.

NOTE "Light" and "regular" coconut milk can be created by diluting the thick coconut milk from the can. (I suggest Chaokoh brand from Thailand, which is available in Asian groceries.) Dilute 1 cup of the (thick) canned coconut milk with 1 cup of warm water, resulting in "light" coconut milk. What I call "regular" coconut milk can be made by diluting the milk from the can with 1/2 cup warm water.

    Some years back I would prepare coconut milk from scratch by opening a brown hard-shelled coconut, removing the white meat, cutting it into thin pieces, combining it with an equal amount of hot water, and processing the mixture in a blender. Then I'd strain the mixture; the liquid was fresh coconut milk. You can discard the pulp or use it in other dishes.

NASI DAGANG #2 (MALAY)

Mixed Rice with Coconut Milk

Here is another type of *nasi dagang* that is served for breakfast in the states of Kelantan and Terengganu on the eastern coast of Malaysia.

1 *cup glutinous rice*
1 *cup long-grain rice*
1½ *teaspoons sugar*
1 *teaspoon salt*
½ *teaspoon fenugreek seed* (halba *in Malay*)
3 *cups "light" coconut milk (see page 14)*
2 *cups "thick" coconut milk (see page 14)*
a 1-inch piece ginger, cut into julienne slices
2 *shallots, sliced*

1. Soak both rices together in water for 3 hours and drain. Steam the rice, covered, over boiling water for 20–25 minutes to soften. Remove from the steamer and mix with sugar, the salt, fenugreek seeds, and "light" coconut milk. Return to the steamer for 10 minutes.

2. Remove again from the steamer, and mix with the "thick" coconut milk, ginger, and shallots.
    Serve warm.

SERVES 8 WITH A FISH CURRY FOR BREAKFAST.

Nasi Goreng Pahang (Malay/Chinese)

Fried Rice from Pahang

Pahang is that large state on the east coast of the Malay peninsula. In Kuantan, the principal city, the fried rice is glorified with shrimp, fish, chicken, and hot chili, among other ingredients. It can be a complete meal, give or take a side dish and soup. It is also a good example of a cross-cultural amalgamation, with both the Chinese and Malays having had a culinary influence on the dish.

2–3 *hot red fresh chilis, or to taste, seeded and sliced*
  4 *shallots, sliced*
  1 *clove garlic, sliced*
1/2 *teaspoon* belacan, *toasted (see Glossary)*
  2 *tablespoons water*
  2 *tablespoons vegetable oil*
1/4 *pound small shrimp, cooked and peeled*
1/4 *pound boneless chicken, cooked and sliced*
  6 *fish balls (page 192), sliced*
1/4 *pound ground fish loaf (available in Chinese markets in the fresh or frozen sections), sliced*
  1 *egg, beaten*
  5 *cups cooked rice, chilled until cold*
  1 *large handful fresh mustard greens (chai sim), leaves only, sliced*
1/2 *teaspoon salt*
1/2 *teaspoon white pepper*

1. Process the chilis, shallots, garlic, and *belacan* with the water to a smooth paste.
2. Heat the oil in a wok or large skillet and stir-fry the shallot paste over moderate heat for 2 minutes. Add the shrimp, chicken, fish balls, and fish loaf and stir-fry for 1 minute.

3. Add the egg and stir it into the mixture for 1 minute. Add the rice, mustard leaves, salt, and pepper and stir-fry to combine all the ingredients.

    Serve hot.

SERVES 8 WITH A SELECTION OF SIDE DISHES.

Nasi Minyak (Malay)

Spiced Celebration Rice

Minyak is not your everyday rice, but one reserved as a special dish for celebrations. It was in the Islamic town of Kuala Kangsar when the two lady cooks from the Sultan's palace were teaching me how to make a royal dish, *Kurma* (page 294), that they told me that this *nasi minyak* was served with it — by the Sultan's wish.

1/4   *cup vegetable oil*
      a 1-inch piece ginger, sliced
4   *shallots, sliced*
4   *cloves garlic, sliced*
6   *cups water*
1/2   *cup evaporated milk*
3   *pandan leaves (see Glossary) or 1/4 teaspoon bottled imitation pandan essence, available in Southeast Asian markets (optional)*
2   *stalks lemongrass, lower 5 inches, cracked*
1   *teaspoon salt, or to taste*
1/2   *cup canned tomato sauce*
4   *cups long-grain rice*
1/4   *cup raisins*
      roasted almonds, crisp fried shallots (see How to Make, page 288), sliced scallions for garnish

1. Heat the oil in a large pan, and in it stir-fry the ginger, shallots, and garlic for 1 minute over low heat. Add the water, and bring it to a boil. Add the milk, pandan if using, lemongrass, salt, tomato sauce, and rice. Bring to a boil.

2. Now add the raisins, cover the pan, and cook over low heat for 20 minutes. Stir once or twice during this cooking time.

    Serve warm, garnished with the almonds, crisp shallots, and scallions.

SERVES 10 WITH ROYAL *KURMA*.

Masala Thosai (Indian)

Stuffed Rice Crepes (Dosa)

There is much more to *masala thosai* than meets the eye by looking at the title of this classic South Indian dish that has been transplanted to Malaysia. My teacher, who was of South Indian origin, was addicted to *thosai* (Malaysian spelling) and used it in one form or another daily.

There are three parts to *thosai:* the crepe, the chutney, and the *sambar,* each one complementing the other. For the complete classic dish, here are three separate recipes that can be used together or separately for other culinary ideas.

Crepe Batter

1½ *cups long-grain rice*
 ½ *cup skinless* urad *(black)* dal
 1 *teaspoon fenugreek seed*
1½ *teaspoons salt, or to taste*
 4 *cups water*

1. Place all the ingredients in a bowl and let them soak overnight at room temperature.
2. The next day, reserve 1½ cups of the soaking water, and drain off the balance. Place the rice mixture with the reserved water in a blender and process until smooth.
3. Put the batter in a large bowl and let it ferment overnight at room temperature. The mixture will develop a thick spongy consistency with a slightly fermented flavor.

    Set aside until ready to fry and stuff crepes.

The Chutney

This is a basic recipe of coconut chutney.

  1 *teaspoon vegetable oil*
 ¹/₂ *teaspoon black mustard seed*
 1–2 *fresh hot green chilis, cut into 3 pieces each, seeded*
  1 *cup grated fresh coconut*
  2 *tablespoons* chana ka dal *(yellow split lentils)*
 ¹/₂ *teaspoon salt*
 ³/₄ *cup water*
 ¹/₂ *teaspoon tamarind paste cleaned of seeds and fibers (use best quality, imported from Thailand)*
  2 *tablespoons fresh coriander leaves*
  2 *teaspoons chopped fresh or dried curry leaves (available in Indian, Thai, and Southeast Asian markets)*

1. Add the oil to a *karai* (wok) or skillet with the mustard seeds and pop them over moderate heat for a few seconds. Add the chilis, coconut, *chana ka dal,* and salt and toast for a minute or two, stirring continuously so that the color of the coconut changes slightly.
2. Transfer the mixture to a blender, add the water, and process to a smooth paste. Add the coriander and curry leaves and blend for ¹/₂ minute to incorporate them into the mixture.

   MAKES ABOUT 1 CUP.

The Sambar

Sambar is usually served with the crepes and chutney. It may be cooked as a vegetarian stew or, by using more water, about 1¹/₂ cups, can be turned into a soup. In which case, as I sometimes do, consciously consider this a soup on its own and act accordingly.

  1 *heaping tablespoon tamarind paste (see ingredients above)*
  1 *taro root (¹/₂ pound peeled), cut into ¹/₂-inch cubes (2 cups)*
 ¹/₂ *cup* chana ka dal, *soaked in water 4 hours and cooked until soft*
  2 *tablespoons* sambar *powder (see How to Make, page 293)*

1   teaspoon black mustard seed, popped in oil (see Step #1, Chutney)
1/2   teaspoon turmeric
1   teaspoon salt, or to taste
1   cup water
1/16 teaspoon, a minute amount, asafetida (hing, see Glossary)
1   teaspoon fresh or dried curry leaves, sliced thin (see above)

1.   Soak the tamarind paste in 1 cup warm water for 1/2 hour,
     strain, reserving the liquid, and discard seeds and fibers.
2.   Bring the reserved tamarind liquid to a boil in a pan with the
     taro, chana ka dal, sambar powder, mustard seeds, turmeric, salt,
     and 1 cup water. Simmer over moderate heat until the taro is
     soft. Add the hing, stir, and add the curry leaves.
        The stew is ready to serve with the crepes and chutney.

SERVES 6

VARIATION Other vegetables may be used instead of taro root, such as 2
     cups red sweet pepper, cut into 1-inch cubes. Whole okra with tip and
     stem trimmed, cauliflower florets, diced carrots, or potatoes cut into
     1/2-inch cubes can also be used, or a mixture of only two or three dif-
     ferent vegetables. You need a total of 2 cups vegetables.

Stuffing the Crepes

The round, black heavy iron griddle about 1/4 inch thick and 12
inches in diameter from India that I saw appears to have been used
in Malayasia for a century. Heated over low heat and very lightly
oiled it became a reliable piece of equipment for frying the crepes. If
you do not have this authentic griddle, a handicraft from south India
that was transported to Malaysia, then a modern Teflon skillet, at
least 14 inches or more in diameter, will be completely serviceable.

1   iron griddle (see above) or Teflon skillet
1   teaspoon corn oil added when needed

1.   Heat the griddle with the oil over moderate/low heat for 2 or 3
     minutes.
2.   Pour in 1/2 cup of the fermented crepe batter. With a metal

spoon, spread the batter from the center of the round outward in concentric circles until the crepe is about 8 to 14 inches in diameter. (It can be any size you wish.) The thinner the crepe, the crispier it will become.

3.   Fry the crepe about ½ minute, then turn it over for another ½ minute, just enough to set the batter and turn it a pale geige color.

Remove and stuff the crepe in the kitchen or serve it with one or more stuffings and let the diners prepare their own stuffed crepes. Leftover batter may be covered and refrigerated, but must be brought back to room temperature before using again.

Stuffing Variations

The fried crepes lend themselves to eclectic treatments. The pancakes have an intrinsic flavor so that they may be stuffed with classic dry vegetarian curries or with sweets. I also like them plain now and then since they are even compatible with western food—scrambled eggs, that sort of thing. But most of the time the crepes are at their best when stuffed and served in the classic South Indian manner.

Sweet Crepes

Warm crepes may be sprinkled with sugar, folded over into half moons, and served at the coffee or tea hour.

Potato-Stuffed Crepes

This is a traditional classic *bhaji*, a dry vegetable curry that is most frequently used. An assortment of vegetables in this curry would always include the potato glorified with bits of cauliflower, green or red pepper, the long Indian string bean known as *loobia*, or any vegetable that suits you.

1   *tablespoon vegetable oil*
½   *cup chopped onion*
1   *teaspoon black mustard seed, popped in oil (see Step #1, Chutney)*

1   *potato (¹/₂ pound), cooked in its skin until soft, peeled, and chopped*
     coarse
¹/₂ *teaspoon salt, or to taste*
1   *or 2 teaspoons storebought curry powder, to taste*
1   *clove garlic, finely chopped*
1   *tablespoon fresh lime juice*

1.   Heat the oil in a *karai* (wok) or skillet, and brown the onion
     over moderate heat for 2 minutes. Add the popped mustard
     seeds, potato, and salt and stir-fry for 2 minutes. Then add the
     curry powder and garlic and continue to stir-fry until all the in-
     gredients are combined.
2.   Let cool slightly, then sprinkle with the lime juice.
     Serve warm or at room temperature as a stuffing for crepes.

ENOUGH STUFFING FOR 4 OR 5 PERSONS.

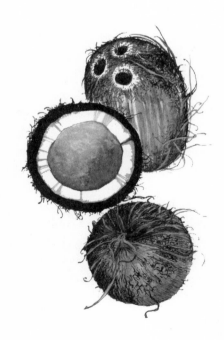

Roti Canai (Indian)

Crisp Fried Pancakes

Roti canai is of Indian origin but has entered the mainstream of Malaysian cooking. Hole-in-the-wall restaurants and food stalls during the breakfast hour prepare *rotis* by the hundreds, the cooks stretching out the dough and flinging it out ever farther and thinner to shape these delectable, filling, crisp pancakes inevitably accompanied by curried chicken gravy and perhaps a cube of potato, along with a cup of strong tea flavored with milk and sugar as it is in India. For many midmorning snacks I followed this familiar scenario all over Malaysia.

1	*cup water*
1/4	*cup milk*
1	*teaspoon sugar*
1/4	*teaspoon salt*
1	*egg, beaten*
3 1/2	*cups flour*
	ghee *(clarified butter) or butter at room temperature*

1. Mix together the water, milk, sugar, salt, and egg in a large bowl. Add the flour and mix well. Knead until you have a soft dough that can be manipulated.
2. Prepare dough balls by tearing off about 3 ounces of the dough, rolling it into a ball, flattening it, and rubbing it with soft *ghee* or butter. (Some cooks use oil but *ghee* is the preferred although more expensive lubricant.) Rub a baking pan with *ghee* and align the balls in rows. Cover the pan with plastic wrap and let stand for 1 day in the refrigerator. Makes 20 balls.
3. The next day, let the dough balls stand at room temperature. Flatten a ball smoothly on a large flat skillet or griddle well lubricated with *ghee* to a diameter of 6 inches. Warm the skillet or griddle over low heat since *rotis* should be fried slowly.

Lift the pancake, place 4 fingers of the left hand on top and the thumb underneath for support. Put 4 fingers of the right hand on the bottom of the pancake and the thumb on top about 4 inches from the left hand.

With a quick movement, throw the right hand over toward the left on to the working table or board. Do this 2 or 3 times to stretch the dough as thin as possible without tearing it, although this is not fatal. (Practice this technique with a kitchen towel so you can become adept at throwing the pancake around.)

4. Fold the stretched pancake over from the right and left sides and from the top and bottom to the center to shape a round 6 inches in diameter. Flatten it out slightly and fry over low heat on both sides until brown and crisp, about 3 or 4 minutes. Make pancakes with the remaining dough in the same manner.

To serve, slap the sides of the fried *roti* to loosen the inner layers. Serve warm, with chicken gravy and a piece of chicken and/or potato.

MAKES ABOUT 20 PANCAKES.

ROTI TELOR (INDIAN)
Egg-Stuffed Pancakes

This is a modification of *roti canai* (see preceding recipe) in which the thinly flattened dough ball is drizzled all over with beaten egg (or half of one), then sprinkled with 2 tablespoons chopped onion. The dough is then folded over as for the *roti canai* and fried as described in the recipe. The egg pancake is a glorification of what is already a delicious and popular concoction. Early-morning people on their way to work often stop off at the food stalls to have egg-stuffed pancakes.

Bihung Goreng (Chinese)
Fried Rice Noodles

This is homecooking at its daily best. There are no complications, just straightforward stir-frying with an enticing number of ingredients.

Chai sim is a common leafy mustard green found in Chinatown in New York City. *Bihun* are thin rice noodles manufactured in China, Taiwan, and Thailand and are found everywhere. The package is frequently marked "Rice Sticks," which means *bihun*.

½   *pound thin rice noodles*
1   *tablespoon vegetable oil*
1   *clove garlic, smashed with the flat side of a cleaver*
2   *eggs, beaten*
½   *cup peeled and deveined small fresh shrimp*
½   *cup shredded cooked chicken*
1   *tablespoon light soy sauce*
¼   *teaspoon salt*
⅛   *teaspoon pepper*
¼   *pound fresh mustard greens* (chai sim), *chopped if large leaves*
1   *cup fresh bean sprouts*
1   *tablespoon crisp fried shallots (see How to Make, page 288)*
2   *scallions, green part only, sliced*

1.   Soak the rice noodles in warm water to cover for 15 minutes. Drain and set aside.
2.   Heat the oil in a wok or large skillet, add the garlic, and stir-fry until brown. Add the eggs and stir-fry over low heat for 1 minute. Then add the shrimp and chicken and stir-fry for 30 seconds.
3.   Now add the noodles, soy sauce, salt, and pepper. Stir in the mustard greens and bean sprouts and stir-fry the mixture for 2 minutes. Garnish with the crispy shallots and sliced scallions.

Serve warm.

SERVES 4 OR 5.

VARIATION This recipe may also be prepared with 1 pound egg noodles. Non-meat-eaters may prepare this as a complete vegetarian meal by omitting the chicken and shrimp and replacing them with vegetables, such as cauliflower florets, string beans, or carrot slices. Blanch each of them before using.

CHAR KOAY TEOW (CHINESE)

Rice Noodle Stir Fry

The title of this, my first lunch and recipe in Penang, should be "Hawker Food in Swatow Lane," since that is where it happened, on a small block with a half dozen hawker's carts, complete restaurants on wheels. Here, among so many other choices, were sliced fresh fruit on ice and ice *kacang,* shaven ice with sweet beans, evaporated milk, and fruit syrup. At 12:30 P.M., the carts opened for business. There were chairs and tables on the other side of the lane. I settled for this rice noodle dish, a large platter for 65¢. Why cook at home!

This was also the first time I had ever heard the expression "sky juice," which was a puzzling ingredient in the recipe. After that I heard it all over Malaysia. It meant "water."

2	*tablespoons vegetable oil*
1	*pound medium shrimp, peeled and deveined*
1	*clove garlic, chopped*
2	*cups fresh bean sprouts*
1	*tablespoon black soy sauce (* kicip *in Malay, see Glossary)*
2	*tablespoons oyster sauce*
2	*teaspoons chili paste (see Note)*
2	*pounds rice noodles,* ¼ *inch wide, cooked*
2	*dried Chinese sausage (available in Asian markets), sliced thin diagonally*
1	*pound cockles (small clams)*
¼	*teaspoon salt*
¼	*teaspoon sugar*
6	*slices ground fish loaf (available in Chinese markets, in the fresh or frozen sections)*
1	*egg, beaten*
1	*tablespoon water*
2	*scallions, green part only, cut into 1-inch pieces*

1. Heat the oil in a wok, add the shrimp, and stir-fry over moderate heat for 2 minutes. Add the garlic, bean sprouts, soy sauce, oyster sauce, chili paste, and noodles and stir-fry for 2 minutes.
2. Now add the sausage, cockles, salt, sugar, and fish loaf and continue to stir-fry until heated through. Lastly, add the egg, fold it in, and cook well. Add the water and scallions and combine well.

Serve warm.

SERVES 6 OR 7.

NOTE Chili paste is a bottled red sauce of hot chilis pulverized with several seasonings. It is a common ingredient in Chinese and Southeast Asian cooking and can be purchased in Chinese groceries.

CURRY MEE (CHINESE)

Curried Egg Noodles

Malaysia is a plural society and it does not surprise me that even the cooking is plural: a Chinese recipe in spite of curry having originated in India. The proof of the pudding is in the eating.

	a 1-inch piece galangal (see Glossary), sliced
5	*shallots, sliced*
1	*teaspoon turmeric*
4	*cloves garlic, sliced*
3	*tablespoons curry powder*
1/4	*cup water*
1/4	*cup corn oil*
10	*cups chicken stock*
4	*stalks lemongrass, bottom 4 inches, cracked*
1	*cup "regular" coconut milk (see page 14)*
1	*teaspoon salt, or to taste*
2	*pounds fresh thin Chinese egg noodles*
2	*cups fresh bean sprouts*
1	*cup cooked and sliced boneless chicken*
1/2	*cup cooked and peeled shrimp*
1/2	*cup lightly cooked, sliced squid*
1/4	*cup fresh mint leaves*

1. Process the galangal, shallots, turmeric, garlic, and curry powder to a smooth paste with the water in a blender.

2. Heat the corn oil in a wok or large skillet and stir-fry the spice paste over low heat for 2 minutes as the aroma rises.

3. Add the chicken stock and lemongrass, bring to a boil over low heat, and simmer for 20 minutes. Add the coconut milk and simmer for 10 minutes more. Add salt to taste. This is the hot curried broth.

4. Blanch the noodles in boiling water for 2 minutes. Blanch the bean sprouts for 1 minute. Drain well.
5. To serve, put portions of the noodles in Chinese soup bowls. Garnish with bean sprouts, chicken, shrimp, squid, and a teaspoon of mint leaves. Pour the hot curried broth over all.

    Serve hot.

SERVES 8.

KUAH TEOW
(KAI SI HOR FUN IN CANTONESE)

Rice Noodles with Chicken and Prawns

My friends in the city of Ipoh, known as the food paradise, have told me that this is the most popular dish in their town. And *kuah teow* is prepared two different ways: (1) as a dry noodle, with just enough sauce to moisten the preparation, and (2) as a soup with the same ingredients served in a bowl with enough hot broth to cover the noodles and a garnish of chicken, prawns, scallions, hot chilis, and crispy shallots.

Note that prawns, as the Malaysians call them, are shrimp as we know them. The size does not influence the word used.

2   *pounds fresh rice noodles, 1/4 inch wide, cooked and still warm*
2   *teaspoons regular soy sauce*
1   *teaspoon black soy sauce (* kicip *in Malay, see Glossary)*
1/4 *cup hot chicken broth*
1   *teaspoon corn oil*
1 1/2 *pounds skinless boneless chicken, cooked and cubed*
1   *pound medium prawns, cooked and peeled*
1/4 *cup crisp fried shallots (see How to Make, page 288)*
3   *scallions, sliced thin*
2   *or 3 fresh hot red chilis, seeded and sliced thin*

1. Stir-fry the warm noodles in a wok with both the soy sauces, hot chicken broth, and oil until combined.
2. Add the chicken, prawns, shallots, scallions, and chilis to taste. Toss until everything is combined well.

    Serve warm or at room temperature.

SERVES 8.

CHICKEN AND OTHER POULTRY

Chicken is the most popular meat in Malaysia, available in markets in the cities and running around loose in the *kampongs* (villages). The Muslims do not eat pork and the Hindus do not eat beef. The Chinese have learned to eat everything and are not restricted by any social pattern. Chicken, therefore, is neutral territory that can be put to use by everyone.

Malaysian chicken recipes are wonderful, both in quantity and variety. The best way to sample them is to search out ethnic restaurants from all of the communities and taste the cook's prowess.

Currying chicken, both with and without the ubiquitous coconut milk that enriches everything it touches, is probably the easiest available method of cooking this popular meat. Hot chilis seem mandatory, along with lemongrass, curry leaves, and curry powders, all of which have a certain popularity, plus tamarind liquid, among other preferred ingredients.

The *rempah*, also called the "four brothers"—star anise, cinnamon stick, cardamom pods, and whole cloves—add their magic to chicken dishes, setting them apart from curries and stews in other countries.

The chicken reigns supreme in the culinary firmament of Malaysia.

Ayam Goreng Bakar Kuah Percik (Malay)

Twice-Cooked Baked Chicken

Ovens are not always available in *kampong* (village) homes or even in larger towns. Frying, barbecuing, boiling, and steaming are methods of cooking. The chicken here is first fried, then baked—for those who have ovens. The sambal that follows this recipe is an important accompaniment.

The Chicken

4   *pounds chicken parts, such as breasts, thighs, and legs, loose skin and fat removed*
1   *teaspoon turmeric*
1   *teaspoon salt, or to taste*
1   *cup vegetable oil*

The Sauce

4   *shallots, sliced*
4   *cloves garlic*
5   *fresh hot red chilis, seeded and sliced*
2   *teaspoons fennel seed or ground powder*
¼   *cup chopped tomato*
2   *teaspoons prepared* kurma *powder (see How to Make, page 294)*
2   *teaspoons sugar*
½   *teaspoon salt*
2   *stalks lemongrass, bottom 5 inches, cracked*
½   *cup "regular" coconut milk (see page 14)*

1.   Prepare the chicken: Mix the chicken, turmeric, and salt together and let stand for 15 minutes.
2.   Heat the oil in a wok or skillet and fry the chicken pieces in

batches on both sides over moderate heat for 5 minutes. Remove and set aside.

3. Make the sauce: Process the shallots, garlic, chilis, fennel seeds,
    tomato, *kurma* powder, sugar, and salt to a smooth paste. Pour
    the sauce over the chicken, add the lemongrass and coconut
    milk, and mix together well.

4. Pour the mixture in a large baking dish and bake in a preheated
    350-degree oven for ½ hour, basting occasionally.

    Serve warm with rice and a fruit and vegetable side dish,
    such as the one that follows.

SERVES 6 TO 8.

Ayam Masak Merah (Malay)

Spicy Red Chicken

Many of the people I cooked with in Malaysia told me they had been cooking with coconut oil since their childhood. Yet these same people were familiar with the information we have about cholesterol. They admitted that imported corn oil (which I call for below) was better, but too expensive. Everything in life is related to money.

1/4   cup tomato purée
1   tablespoon chili boh (see How to Make, page 290)
      a 1/2-inch piece ginger, sliced
4   cloves garlic, sliced
4   shallots, sliced
1   medium onion, sliced (1/2 cup)
1/2   teaspoon salt
2   tablespoons water
1/4   cup corn oil
      a 3-pound chicken, cut into 8 pieces, skin and fat removed
2   stalks lemongrass, bottom 5 inches, cracked
1/2   cup "regular" coconut milk (see page 14)

1.   Process the tomato purée, chili paste, ginger, garlic, shallots, onion, and salt with the water to a smooth paste.
2.   Heat the oil in a large pan, add the spice paste, and fry it over low heat for 5 minutes. Add the chicken pieces and lemongrass and mix well. Cover, and cook over low heat for 15 minutes.
3.   Add the coconut milk and simmer until the chicken is tender, another 15 minutes. Adjust the salt, if necessary.
      Serve warm with rice.

SERVES 8, WITH OTHER DISHES.

SAMBAL

Side Dish

Sambal is a spicey sidedish that goes especially well with chicken.

½ cup sliced cucumber
½ cup pineapple cubes
½ cup tomato cubes
½ cup carrot slices
1 tablespoon white vinegar
1 teaspoon sugar
¼ teaspoon salt
2 tablespoons roasted peanuts
1 fresh red or green chili, seeded and sliced thin
1 small onion, sliced into rings

1. Mix the vegetables and fruit together in a bowl.
2. In a small bowl stir together the vinegar, sugar, and salt.
3. Stir the vinegar sauce into the vegetables and fruit. Garnish with the peanuts, chilis, and onion rings.
    Serve at room temperature with Ayam Goreng Bakar.

KURMA (MALAY)

Spiced Chicken with Lime

I was sitting in the lobby of my hotel in Ipoh one morning. The monsoon rains were at their fiercest, with violent wind prohibiting long walks in the town. A Malay gentleman suggested that I visit the royal town of Kuala Kangsar, formerly the resident palace of the Sultan but no longer. He told me that if I appeared in the town at seven in the evening he would introduce me to two lady cooks (retired) from the palace. I did, he did, and the ladies taught me two royal recipes. Surprisingly, there is no chili in this *kurma,* only in the garnish.

	a 1¹/₂-inch piece cinnamon stick
1	*whole star anise*
¹/₂	*teaspoon ground fennel*
5	*cardamom pods*
5	*shallots*
5	*cloves garlic*
	a 1-inch piece ginger
1¹/₂	*tablespoons blanched almonds*
³/₄	*cup water*
1	*pound potatoes (2 large), peeled and cut into 1-inch cubes*
	a 3¹/₂-pound chicken, loose skin and fat removed, cut into 8 pieces
1	*teaspoon salt, or to taste*
2	*cups "regular" coconut milk (see page 14)*
1	*medium onion, sliced thin, for garnish*
8	*fresh hot green chilis, for garnish*
2	*limes, quartered, for garnish*

1. Process the cinnamon stick, star anise, fennel, cardamom pods, shallots, garlic, ginger, and almonds to a smooth paste with the water in a blender. Transfer the paste to a pan, bring to a boil,

and add the potato, chicken, salt, and the coconut milk. Cover the pan and simmer over low heat for ½ hour, or until the chicken is tender and the sauce has thickened.

Serve warm garnished with the onion, chilis, and limes.

SERVES 6 WITH RICE.

Gulai Ayam Bendir (Malay)

Chicken Curry with Okra

One of my all-time favorite vegetables is okra, or lady fingers, as it is called in the British Empire. My attraction to okra occurred during the years I spent in India and has not diminished. It was intensified once again in Malaysia with this curry. I noticed that the okra around the Malaysian countryside was substantially longer than elsewhere. Also, it was often employed as a garnish rather than as an intrinsic ingredient in the dish being prepared.

4   *shallots, sliced*
3   *cloves garlic, sliced*
2   *tablespoons curry powder*
2   *cups "regular" coconut milk (see page 14)*
1   *tablespoon vegetable oil*
3   *lobes star anise*
3   *whole cloves*
    a 3-inch cinnamon stick
3   *pounds chicken parts (12 pieces), loose skin and fat removed*
1   *teaspoon salt, or to taste*
8   *okras, top and bottom trimmed by about ¼ inch*

1. Process the shallots, garlic, and curry powder with ½ cup of the coconut milk to a smooth paste in a blender.

2. Heat the oil in a large skillet, add the spice paste, star anise, cloves, and cinnamon stick, and stir-fry over low heat for 3 minutes.

3. Add the chicken, cover the pan, and cook over low heat for 5 minutes. Add the balance of the coconut milk and salt and bring the liquid to a boil. Simmer for 20 minutes, stirring now and then. When the chicken is tender and the sauce thickened, add the okra and cook, covered, for 5 minutes more.

    Serve warm with rice and any side dish.

SERVES 6 OR MORE.

Rendang Ayam (Malay)

Dry Spiced Chicken Roast

This is a top-of-the-stove dry roast chicken with a battery of spices in the Malay fashion. The chicken pieces should be moist, but there is no sauce.

1	*tablespoon vegetable oil*
5	*shallots, sliced*
	a 2-inch piece ginger, peeled and sliced
2	*stalks lemongrass, bottom 5 inches, cracked*
1/4	*cup fresh tomato slices (2 or 3)*
1	*pandan leaf (optional, see Glossary)*
5	*fresh or dried curry leaves (available in Indian, Thai, and Southeast Asian markets)*
1	*teaspoon tomato paste*
1	*tablespoon curry powder*
1/2	*cup "regular" coconut milk (see page 14)*
3	*pounds chicken parts, such as breasts and thighs, cut into 18 pieces*
2	*large potatoes (1 pound), peeled and cut into 1-inch cubes*
1/2	*teaspoon salt*

1. Heat the oil in a pan, add the shallots, ginger, lemongrass, tomato slices, pandan leaf if using, and curry leaves and stir-fry over low heat for 2 minutes. Add the tomato paste and curry powder and mix together well.

2. Add the coconut milk, chicken, potatoes, and salt and stir-fry the mixture for 3 minutes. Cover the pan and cook over low heat for 25 minutes, enough time to tenderize the chicken and cook off most of the liquid. Adjust the salt.

   Serve warm with rice.

SERVES 8.

Ayam Percek (Malay)

Barbecued and Basted Chicken

Barbecue has been absorbed into the backyards of a number of cultures. In one way or another, primitive man's solution for simple cooking has been translated into building a wood or charcoal fire, seasoning meat, and placing it over the heat to cook. In this case, *ayam percek* is precooked over charcoal (ideally), then basted with a thick, vivid sauce until the chicken parts are crusty and have absorbed the flavors as well as the pungent smoke of the barbecue.

2½ *pounds chicken parts, such as breasts and thighs, with or without bone*
1 *teaspoon salt*
1 *teaspoon turmeric*
2 *cloves garlic, smashed with the flat side of a cleaver*
2 *slices ginger, smashed with the flat side of a cleaver*

The Basting Sauce

1½ *cups "regular" coconut milk (see page 14)*
1 *medium onion, sliced (½ cup)*
2 *stalks lemongrass, root end bulb only, sliced*
   a ½-inch piece galangal (see Glossary), sliced
1 *tablespoon dried chili flakes, moistened with water*
1 *tablespoon tamarind paste dissolved in ¼ cup water, strained (see How to Make, page 289)*
1 *teaspoon sugar*

1. Score each chicken part with 2 diagonal cuts on each side.
2. Mix the salt, turmeric, garlic, and ginger together. Rub this into the incisions on the chicken. Set aside for ½ hour.
3. Prepare the basting sauce: In a food processor combine the coconut milk, onion, lemongrass, galangal, chili flakes, tamarind liquid, and sugar and process until smooth. Transfer the sauce

to a pan and simmer over low heat for about 20 minutes, until it thickens. Adjust the salt and sugar according to taste.

4.   Grill the chicken parts over charcoal or in a gas or electric oven broiler, turning them now and then, for about 10 minutes. Brush the basting sauce over the chicken and continue to grill. Baste several times to intensify the flavors. Total grilling and basting time is about 20 minutes, or until you are satisfied that the chicken is cooked through.

Serve warm with other Malaysian dishes.

SERVES 4 TO 6.

Ayam Goreng Berkunyit (Malay)

Chicken Liver Tidbits

This dish is well seasoned, in Malay style, which here also includes bits of fresh hot red chili. An ideal accompaniment to drinks.

1	*pound whole chicken livers*
1/2	*teaspoon salt*
1/2	*teaspoon white pepper*
1/2	*teaspoon turmeric*
1/4	*cup vegetable oil for pan frying*
1	*medium onion, sliced into rings (1/2 cup)*
3	*fresh hot red chilis, seeded and sliced lengthwise into thirds*

1. Rinse the chicken livers in cold water and pat them dry. Season with the salt, pepper, and turmeric and toss to coat.
2. Heat the oil in a wok or skillet, add the livers, and stir-fry over moderate heat for 3 minutes. Remove from the oil with a slotted spoon.
3. Add the onion rings and chilis to the wok and stir-fry for 1 minute. Return the livers to the pan and stir-fry the mixture for 2 more minutes. Adjust the salt if necessary.

    Serve warm.

SERVES 6 TO 8 AS AN APPETIZER WITH DRINKS OR
AS A SIDE DISH WITH OTHER FOODS.

GULAI TELOR (MALAY)

Poached Egg Curry

This is a variation on Tuna Fish Curry (page 119) and is considered a breakfast or luncheon dish, which may or may not be served with Nasi Dagang #1.

1   *recipe sauce (steps 1 and 2 in Tuna Fish Curry)*
8   *eggs*

1.   Prepare the curry sauce in a large skillet and simmer it slowly over low heat for 10 minutes. Remove the skillet from the heat and break the eggs, spacing them evenly, very carefully into the sauce.
2.   Return the pan to the heat and simmer over low heat for 4 minutes for soft poached eggs or 6 minutes for a more well-cooked texture.

   Serve warm with rice and side dishes.

SERVES 8.

Kari Puyuh (Malay)

Curried Quail

Reputed to enhance the virility of men, domesticated quail are sweet, tender, and especially good enrobed in a local curry sauce. Curry powder is used in every city I visited, but my Kedah cook in Alor Setar admitted that one had more control over the flavor by mixing one's own combination.

Thursday is market day in Alor Setar, Kedah state. A rather large group of women with a sprinkling of men sets up their green and white umbrellas in a downtown parking lot. Cooked food is brought in with fruit, vegetables, and some meat from their *kampong* (village). Conspicuous in November was corn on the cob, longbeans (*loobia*), extra-long okra, herbs, and various sizes of red shallots. Women shoppers, wearing their long traditional colorful dress with head scarf, thronged the paths around the stalls.

One visitor brought in an impressive heap of quail.

1   *medium onion, sliced (²/₃ cup)*
3   *shallots, sliced*
2   *cloves garlic, sliced*
1   *scallion, sliced thin*
3   *tablespoons water, plus 1 cup*
3   *tablespoons vegetable oil*
2   *tablespoons hot red chili powder*
1   *tablespoon curry powder*
10 *fresh or dried curry leaves (available in Indian, Thai, and Southeast Asian markets)*
    a 3-inch cinnamon stick
3   *lobes star anise*
4   *good-size quail, cleaned and rinsed*
¹/₂ *cup "regular" coconut milk (see page 14)*
¹/₄ *teaspoon sugar*
¹/₄ *teaspoon salt*

1. Process the onion, shallots, garlic, and scallion to a smooth paste with the 3 tablespoons water to moisten the mixture.
2. Heat the oil in a pan or wok, add the onion paste, chili powder, curry powder, curry leaves, cinnamon stick, and star anise and stir-fry over low heat for 10 minutes as the aroma rises.
3. Add the 1 cup water and mix well. Put the quail into the curry and simmer for 15 to 20 minutes, or until they are tender. Add the coconut milk, sugar, and salt and simmer over low heat for 5 minutes. Do not let the coconut milk boil rapidly since it has a tendency to separate.

    Serve warm.

    SERVES 4 WITH RICE AND SIDE DISHES.

NOTE The same curry may be made using 2 Cornish game hens weighing about 1 pound each. Know that the cooking time above should be extended to tenderize the hens.

EGG CURRY WITH VEGETABLES (MALAY)

This egg curry is from Malacca and is subject to the different regional methods of preparing the same dish. It is a curry that is often an adjunct to others in the same meal, primarily for those dedicated vegetarians who have eliminated meat and fish from their diets.

4	*shallots, sliced*
4	*cloves garlic, sliced*
	a 1/2-inch piece ginger, sliced
1/4	*cup water*
3	*tablespoons vegetable oil*
2	*tablespoons curry powder*
1/2	*pound potatoes (2), peeled and cut into 1/2-inch cubes*
2	*medium carrots, peeled and sliced on the diagonal (1 cup)*
1	*cup "regular" coconut milk (see page 14)*
6	*hard-cooked eggs, peeled*
2–3	*fresh hot green chilis, seeded and sliced*
1/2	*pound Oriental eggplant (1), cut into 1-inch cubes*
1	*teaspoon salt*
1	*ripe medium tomato, cut into 1/2-inch cubes*
2	*tablespoons tamarind paste dissolved in 1/2 cup water, strained (see How to Make, page 289)*

1. Process the shallots, garlic, and ginger with the water to a smooth paste.

2. Heat the oil in a pan, add the garlic paste, and stir-fry over low heat for 2 minutes as the aroma rises. Stir in the curry powder as the paste cooks.

3. Add the potatoes and carrots, cover the pan, and simmer for 5 minutes. Add the coconut milk, eggs, chilis, eggplant, salt, tomato, and tamarind liquid and mix well.

4.   Cover the pan and simmer over low heat for 10 minutes, long enough to soften all the vegetables and integrate the flavors. Serve warm with rice.

SERVES 6.

TELOR DADAR (MALAY)

Spiced Omelette

I had heard through the hotel grapevine in Alor Setar that an eating shop (restaurant) in a nearby *kampong* called Pum Pung was serving a large variety of Malay foods, so off I went with a Chinese chef. At about noon the kitchen staff began to bring out foods—large pans of soups, rice, vegetable stews, fish curries, fried chicken and quail, among many—and put them on a stand. There was a crush of people from the street who selected what they wanted from an assortment of about twenty-five different traditional dishes, paid for what they took, and sat down at the tables. Among the assortment was this omelette.

2	*tablespoons vegetable oil*
8	*eggs, beaten*
2	*medium onions, sliced into thin rings (1 cup)*
2	*or 3 fresh hot red chilis, seeded and sliced thin*
1	*teaspoon salt*
⅛	*teaspoon white pepper*

Heat the oil in a large skillet. Mix the eggs and all the remaining ingredients together and pour the mixture into the pan. Fry the omelette over moderate heat until light brown on both sides.

Serve warm, sliced like a pie, for lunch.

SERVES 4 TO 6.

CHOW SIEW (CHINESE)

Barbecued Chicken

Here is another "local" recipe from Kuantan. It is simple to prepare and most useful in the American kitchen for sandwiches and salads, or to have with drinks for visiting guests.

The Chinese in Malaysia are sensitive to Islamic values and have transferred the original recipe for roast pork into breast of chicken, an entirely successful substitution.

2 *tablespoons sugar*
1 *tablespoon sesame oil*
⅛ *teaspoon red vegetable food coloring for meat and poultry (available in Chinese markets)*
1 *teaspoon salt*
2 *teaspoons black soy sauce* (kicip, *see Glossary*)
⅛ *teaspoon ground cinnamon*
1 *boneless chicken breast (about 1 pound)*

1. Mix all the seasoning ingredients together, add the chicken breast, and marinate it for 4 hours at room temperature.
2. Put the chicken in an aluminum foil-lined dish and roast in a preheated 325-degree oven for 20 minutes. Remove, let cool, and slice when ready to serve.

    Serve with Nasi Ayam Hailamise (page 54).

SERVES 6 OR MORE.

Nasi Ayam (Chinese)

Chicken Rice

Is this one of the most popular Chinese dishes in Malaysia? Probably, since it is one of the easiest to order for the fast-food contingent that is munching all day and into the night, until midnight often with their children in tow. This is a recipe from Malacca and might be different from the same recipe in other regions even though the name is nationally known.

The Rice

 2   *teaspoons vegetable oil*
 1/4 *cup chopped onion*
 1/2 *teaspoon chopped ginger*
 1   *clove garlic, chopped*
 1   *cup long-grain rice, well rinsed and drained*
 1 1/2 *cups hot chicken broth*
 1/2 *teaspoon salt*
     a 3-inch pandan leaf (optional, see Glossary)

The Chicken

 6   *cups water*
     a 3-pound whole chicken, loose skin and fat removed
 1/2 *teaspoon salt*
     Soy sauce, to taste

1. Prepare the rice: Heat the oil in a pan, add the onion, ginger, and garlic, and stir-fry over low heat for 1 minute. Add the rice and continue to fry for another 2 minutes as the rice changes color.

2. Add the broth, salt, and pandan leaf if using and bring to a boil. Cover the pan, reduce the heat to very low, and cook until the

rice has absorbed all the broth, about 12 minutes. Give the mixture a quick stir to fluff the rice, cover the pan again, and remove from the heat. Let the rice rest to steam in its own heat for 10 minutes before serving.

3. Prepare the chicken: Bring the water to a boil, add the chicken and salt, and simmer over low heat for ½ hour, or until the chicken is tender but not overcooked. Remove, let cool, and discard the skin and fat. Cut the chicken into 1-inch cubes, with or without the bone.

4. To serve, put a portion of rice in a rice bowl. Turn it over on a serving plate. Cover the rice with cubes of boneless chicken. Sprinkle with soy sauce to taste.

    Serve at room temperature with a dish of peeled, sliced cucumbers.

SERVES 4 TO 6.

VARIATION Simply roasted chicken may be served instead of the boiled chicken.

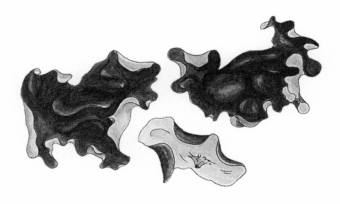

Nasi Ayam Hailamise (Chinese)

Chicken and Rice from Hailam

This is what is known as a "local" recipe from the Chinese who live in the city of Kuantan in eastern Malaysia but originally came from the Hailam Islands in the South China Sea. It is traditional cooking from this community and different from the Chinese in other Malaysian regions.

The Rice

⅓	cup chicken fat
3	shallots, chopped
3	cloves garlic, chopped
4	cups chicken broth
1	teaspoon salt, or to taste
3	pandan leaves (optional, see Glossary)
	a 2-inch piece young ginger, smashed with the flat side of a cleaver
2	cups long-grain rice, rinsed well

The Chicken

8	cups water
	a 3-pound chicken, loose skin and fat removed

The Sauce

¼	cup light soy sauce
¼	cup chicken broth
1	tablespoon sesame oil
1	tablespoon oyster sauce
½	teaspoon sugar

The Garnishes

2   young cucumbers, sliced
4   tomatoes, sliced
     Fresh coriander

The Dipping Sauce

4   fresh hot red chilis, seeded and sliced
     a 2-inch piece young ginger, sliced
4   cloves garlic, sliced
     juice of 1 green lime (about 3 tablespoons)
1   teaspoon sugar
1/2 teaspoon salt
1/4 cup chicken broth

1.   Prepare the rice: Heat the chicken fat in a pan until melted. Discard the brown pieces, and use only the melted fat.
2.   Add the shallots and garlic and stir-fry until light brown. Add the chicken broth and salt and bring to a boil. Add the pandan leaves if using, ginger, and rice.

     (At this stage, you may put the rice mixture into a rice cooker and complete the cooking following the machine instructions. Or, continue to cook the rice in the original pan by bringing the mixture to a boil, reducing the heat to low, covering the pan, and simmering it slowly for 20 minutes.)
3.   Prepare the chicken: Bring the water to a boil, add the chicken, and cook, covered, over low heat for 1/2 hour. Remove the chicken and plunge it into cold water. Let it cool. Cut into about 20 pieces with the bone. Or, bone the chicken, removing the breast, thighs, and legs. Then slice thin.
4.   To serve, line the bottom of a serving platter with the cucumbers. Ring the edge of the platter with the tomatoes. Cover the platter with the sliced chicken and garnish with the coriander leaves.
5.   Prepare the sauce: Mix everything together. Dribble the sauce over the chicken on the serving platter to keep the pieces moist.

6. Prepare the dipping sauce: Process everything together to a smooth sauce. Serve with the chicken and rice.

THE TOTAL SERVING FOR 8 PERSONS WILL CONSIST OF A SEPARATE BOWL OF RICE, WITH THE PLATTER OF CHICKEN, CUCUMBERS, AND TOMATO AND THE SAUCE COVERING ALL. THE DIPPING SAUCE IS SERVED SEPARATELY, WITH THE CHICKEN, TO EMPHASIZE ITS SEASONINGS.

Fa Bo Biu Heong (Chinese)

Monk's Hat (Yam Basket)

This highly dramatic Malaysian dish is not often seen on restaurant menus. The Asiatic yam *(D. alata* or *D. esculenta),* as seen in Chinatowns in many countries, is a large football-shaped tuber with a rough brown skin. The pulp is whitish and consists mainly of starch. It is *not* a sweet potato as we see it in supermarkets, nor should it be confused with one.

The yam here is steamed, mashed, and seasoned for preparation in what looks like a raised monk's hat, but what more accurately is called yam basket.

The Basket

1½ *pounds yam, peeled, halved lengthwise, and sliced thin*
6 *tablespoons flour*
4 *tablespoons corn oil*
2 *tablespoons sugar*
⅛ *teaspoon Chinese five-spice powder*
  vegetable oil for deep frying

The Filling

1 *tablespoon corn oil*
3 *tablespoons cubed green pepper (½-inch cubes)*
½ *cup cubed onions*
3 *dried black mushrooms, soaked in water to cover until softened, drained, and each cut into 4 slices*
2 *ears baby corn, cut into 1-inch pieces*
3 *water chestnuts, sliced thin*
½ *pound cooked chicken, cut into ½-inch cubes*
2 *tablespoons diced carrot (¼-inch dice)*
1 *tablespoon oyster sauce*

1   *tablespoon soy sauce*
¹/₄ *teaspoon sugar*
2   *tablespoons roasted cashew nuts*

1.   Prepare the basket: Steam the yam slices, covered, over boiling water until soft, about 15 minutes. Cool and mash. Add the flour, the oil, sugar, and five-spice powder and combine well.
2.   Make a large doughnut shape, about 3 inches high and 6 inches in diameter, with your fingers.
3.   Heat vegetable oil for deep frying in a wok or deep skillet and put the yam basket in the oil over moderate heat. Brown all over, about 4 minutes. Remove the firm, crisp basket and drain on paper kitchen towels.
4.   Prepare the filling: Heat the oil in a wok, add the green pepper and onions, and stir-fry over moderate heat for 2 minutes. Add the mushrooms, corn, water chestnuts, chicken, and carrot and continue to stir-fry until combined. Lastly, add the oyster sauce, soy sauce, and sugar and toss well.
5.   Pour the hot filling into the prepared yam basket and garnish with the cashews.
    Serve warm.

SERVES 8 WITH OTHER DISHES.

Variation: Here is another method in preparing the Yam Basket.

2¹/₂ *pounds Asiatic yam (sometimes incorrectly called taro), peeled, halved*
    lengthwise, sliced thin
1 *teaspoon salt*
1 *tablespoon sugar*
1 *cup wheat starch or rice flour (purchased Chinese groceries)*
2 *cups vegetable oil*

1.   Put the yam slices into a Chinese-style steamer over hot water and steam until soft, about 15 minutes. Cool and mash with the salt and sugar.
2.   Mix the wheat starch by adding enough hot water, about ¹/₃ cup, little by little to make a moist dough. Knead the starch mixture into the mashed yam.

3. Roll out 2 or 3 strips of yam dough 3 inches wide, ½ inch thick, and 8 inches long. Fold them around with your fingers into a circle 8 inches in diameter, creating a basket. Chill this yam basket in the refrigerator for ½ hour.

4. Heat the oil in a skillet or wok and fry the yam basket until it is brown on all sides, like a doughnut. It will expand slightly. Remove and drain the basket on a kitchen towel.

5. Use the same ingredients for the stuffing as in the first recipe, but replace the ½ pound of cooked chicken with ½ pound of medium-size cooked shrimp. All other instructions are the same.

AYAM KOFTA (IPOH CHINESE)

Chicken Meatballs in Sauce

There are very few Malaysian recipes where chicken, beef, or lamb is ground. This is one, an Ipoh recipe, presumably traditional, but with a double influence of Malay and Indian. So I present it as a very tasty spiced chicken ball recipe, without complete assurance of its community origin.

3 *pounds ground chicken*
1 *teaspoon salt, or to taste*
1/8 *teaspoon pepper*
2 *eggs, beaten*
1/4 *cup corn oil*
4 *shallots, sliced*
4 *cloves garlic, sliced*
   a 2-inch piece young ginger, sliced
2 *teaspoons hot red chili powder*
2 *stalks lemongrass, bottom 5 inches, cracked*
5 *fresh or frozen curry leaves (available in Indian, Thai, and Southeast Asian markets)*
1/4 *teaspoon ground fennel*
1/4 *teaspoon ground coriander*
1/4 *teaspoon ground cumin*
2 *lobes star anise*
   a 1-inch piece cinnamon stick
3 *tablespoons curry powder*
3 *cardamom pods*
2 *cups "regular" coconut milk (see page 14)*

1. Mix the chicken, salt, pepper, and eggs together well. Shape balls 1 1/4 inches in diameter. Makes about 25 balls.
2. Heat the oil in a large skillet and brown the balls in batches over low heat for about 3 minutes. Remove and set aside.

3. In the same oil, stir-fry the shallots, garlic, ginger, chili powder, lemongrass, and curry leaves over low heat for 3 minutes. As you stir-fry, add the fennel, coriander, cumin, star anise, cinnamon stick, curry powder, and cardamom pods and combine well.

4. Add the coconut milk and bring to a boil. Simmer the sauce over low heat for 5 minutes to integrate the flavors. Add the meatballs and simmer 5 minutes more. Do not stir but shake the pan while the meatballs warm through.

  Serve warm.

SERVES 8 WITH RICE.

MALAYSIAN CHICKEN CURRY (INDIAN)

This is a preeminent curry that should be a standard for other curries in Southeast Asia. It is south Indian in origin, since most of the Indians living in Malaysia are of south Indian ancestry. But the coconut milk, star anise, and poppy seeds in it reveal the modifications that occur when geography has changed the milieu and local habits exert an influence on the cooking. The list of spices and seasonings is a vivid illustration of how far the cook will go to develop nuances in the taste. One last thought: The six curry leaves in it are edible.

3 *tablespoons vegetable oil*
   a 3-inch piece cinnamon stick
3 *whole star anise*
3 *whole cloves*
3 *cardamom pods*
3 *medium onions, sliced thin (1½ cups)*
4 *cloves garlic, crushed*
   a 1-inch piece ginger, smashed with the flat side of a cleaver
3 *pounds boneless chicken parts, cut into 2-inch cubes*
1 *large potato (½ pound), peeled and cut into 8 cubes*
2 *tablespoons hot red chili powder, or to taste*
2 *tablespoons ground cumin*
2 *tablespoons ground poppy seed* (khus khus)
1 *tablespoon ground fennel*
1 *tablespoon ground coriander*
1 *teaspoon turmeric*
1 *teaspoon salt, or to taste*
½ *teaspoon white pepper*
1 *tablespoon tomato paste*
1 *cup water*
1 *cup "regular" coconut milk (see page 14)*

6   *fresh or frozen curry leaves (available in Indian, Thai, and Southeast Asian markets)*

1.   Heat the oil in a large pan, spreading it to cover the bottom and sides. Over low heat add the cinnamon stick, star anise, cloves, and cardamom pods and stir-fry for a few seconds as the spices pop. Add the onions and stir-fry until light brown and distinct in flavor. Add the garlic and ginger and toss well.
2.   Add the chicken and potato and stir-fry for 3 minutes. Add the chili powder, cumin, poppy seeds, fennel, coriander, turmeric, salt, white pepper, and tomato paste and combine well.
3.   Add the water, coconut milk, and curry leaves, bring to a boil, cover, and cook over low heat for about ½ hour, long enough for the chicken to tenderize and the sauce to thicken.
     Serve with white rice and side dishes.

SERVES 8.

NOTE This curry is especially recommended for serving with Roti Canai (page 24) and Roti Telor (page 26).

Ayam Masak Mehra Ros (Indian Muslim)

Spicy Tomato Chicken

Not every Indian dish needs to be chili-hot, and this one isn't. What it does have is a combination of spices and seasonings that re-inforce the flavor of the chicken without overwhelming it. That is what this chicken dish fulfills.

The Chicken

3   tablespoons vegetable oil
3   pounds chicken parts, cut into 3-inch pieces, skin and fat removed
1/4   teaspoon turmeric
1   teaspoon salt, or to taste
1   teaspoon hot red chili powder or flakes

The Sauce

1   medium onion, sliced (1/2 cup)
   a 2-inch piece ginger, sliced
1   clove garlic
1   cup water
1   cup canned or homemade tomato sauce
2   teaspoons sugar

1. Prepare the chicken: Heat the oil in a wok or large skillet, add the chicken, turmeric, salt, and chili powder, and stir-fry over low heat for 5 minutes. Remove and set aside.
2. Prepare the sauce: Process the onion, ginger, garlic, and 1/4 cup of the water into a smooth paste.
3. Heat the wok or skillet again, add the onion/ginger paste, and stir-fry it over low heat for 3 minutes, or until the onion turns

golden. Add the tomato sauce, sugar, and balance of the water and bring to a boil.

4. Add the reserved fried chicken, toss well, cover the pan, and simmer the chicken in the sauce for 25 minutes, or until it is tender and the sauce has thickened. Adjust the salt.

Serve warm with rice or Roti Canai (page 24) and side dishes.

SERVES 4 TO 6.

Ayam Kari Kapitan (Nonya)

Captain's Chicken Curry

There are the Nonya of Malacca and the Nonya of Penang, each with different regional styles of cooking. This is a celebrated Nonya Penang curry with its own mythology. It seems that a ship's captain during the early colonial days was staying at a hotel and asked for a special curry, having tired of the ones he had tasted during previous trips. The cook produced this curry, which remained forever more *kari kapitan.*

	a 1-inch piece galangal (see Glossary), sliced
6	*shallots, sliced*
2	kemiri *(macadamia nuts)*
5	*stalks lemongrass, bottom 4 inches, white part, sliced thin*
5	*cloves garlic, sliced*
2	*medium onions, sliced (1 cup)*
1/2	*teaspoon turmeric*
4	*dried hot red chilis*
1	*teaspoon* belacan, *toasted (see Glossary)*
1	*teaspoon salt, or to taste*
1	*teaspoon sugar*
1/4	*teaspoon pepper*
1/4	*cup water*
1/3	*cup vegetable oil*
3	*pounds boneless chicken parts, such as breasts and thighs*
3	*kaffir lime leaves (available at Southeast Asian markets)*
2	*cups chicken broth*
1/2	*cup "thick" coconut milk (see page 14)*
1	*tablespoon lemon juice*
1/4	*cup mint leaves, for garnish*

1. Process the galangal, shallots, *kemiri,* lemongrass, garlic, onions, turmeric, dried chilis, *belacan,* salt, sugar, and pepper with the water to moisten to a smooth paste.

2. Heat the oil in a wok or large pan, add the spice paste, and stir-fry it over low heat for about 10 minutes as the aroma and the oil rise. Pour off all but 1 tablespoon of the spiced oil.

3. Add the chicken pieces, lime leaves, and chicken broth, bring to a boil, and simmer over low heat for 20 minutes. Add the coconut milk and lemon juice and simmer over low heat for 10 minutes more. The chicken should now be tender and the sauce thickened. Garnish with the mint leaves.

Serve warm with steamed rice.

SERVES 8 WITH OTHER DISHES.

Ayam Buah Keluak
(Nonya of Malacca)

Chicken and Pork Curry

I went to the Portuguese settlement on the outskirts of Malacca city at the edge of the Straits of Malacca. The settlement is a quiet enclave of the Nonya community, people who are a product of Chinese/Malay intermarriage with, in this case, Portuguese ancestors of the sixteenth century. Their cuisine is a reflection of this unique background.

3	*medium onions, sliced (1½ cups)*
2–3	*tablespoons hot red dried chilis, to taste*
10	kemiri *(macadamia nuts)*
1	*teaspoon* belacan, *toasted (see Glossary)*
1	*teaspoon turmeric*
	a 1-inch piece galangal (see Glossary), sliced
1	*teaspoon salt, or to taste*
3	*tablespoons water*
¼	*cup vegetable oil*
1½	*pounds chicken parts, cut into 2-inch pieces, with or without bone*
1½	*pounds boneless pork, cut into 1-inch cubes*
4	*stalks lemongrass, bottom 5 inches, cracked*
⅓	*cup tamarind paste soaked in 2 cups water ½ hour, strained (see How to Make, page 289)*

1. Process the onions, chilis, *kemiri, belacan,* turmeric, galangal, and salt to a smooth paste with the water.

2. Heat the oil in a wok or large pan, add the spice paste, and stir-fry over low heat for 2 minutes until the aroma rises. Add the chicken and pork and stir well. Add the lemongrass and tamarind liquid and bring to a boil. Cover the pan and simmer over low heat for 35 minutes, or until the meats are tender and a thick sauce has developed. (If the liquid evaporates

too quickly, add another ½ cup water.) Adjust the salt if necessary.

Serve warm.

SERVES 8 WITH RICE.

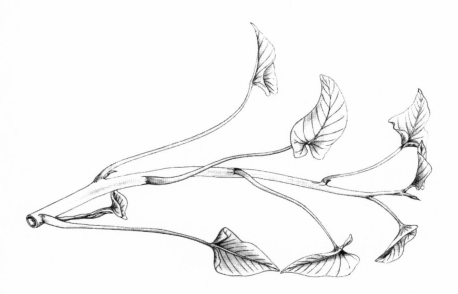

DEBAL KARI AYAM (PORTUGUESE)

Chili-Hot Devil Curry

The city of Malacca is the center of the Portuguese colonial community and their cuisine. The Portuguese captured the city in 1511, so it is logical to figure that the cuisine started after that date. The Portuguese are different from almost everyone else around them and are racially Eurasian, and their food has an almost excessive reliance on the hot chili, fresh and dried. Vinegar also increases the heat. (I learned this during my residence in Calcutta.) Somehow, it all comes together in a unique spice-ridden attractive concoction, like the one below.

5	*dried hot red chilis, soaked in* $^1/_4$ *cup hot water for 15 minutes*
2	*fresh hot red chilis, seeded and sliced*
	a 2-inch piece ginger, sliced
2	*cloves garlic, sliced*
5	*shallots, sliced*
	a 1-inch piece galangal (see Glossary), sliced
6	*kemiri (macadamia nuts)*
$1^1/_4$	*cups chicken stock*
4	*tablespoons vegetable oil*
1	*teaspoon mustard seed, crushed*
4	*pounds chicken parts, cut into about 30 pieces, skin removed*
2	*stalks lemongrass, bottom 5 inches, cracked*
3	*tablespoons rice vinegar*
1	*tablespoon black soy sauce* (kicip *in Malay, see Glossary*)
1	*teaspoon salt, or to taste*
1	*potato, peeled and cut into 1-inch cubes (1$^1/_2$ cups)*
1	*fresh hot red chili, halved lengthwise and seeded*
1	*ripe tomato, cut into cubes (1 cup)*

1. Process the dried chilis and their soaking liquid, the fresh chilis, ginger, garlic, shallots, galangal, *kemiri,* and $^1/_4$ cup of the chicken stock to a smooth paste.

2.   Heat the oil in a large pan and stir-fry the spice paste over moderate heat for 2 minutes. Add the mustard seeds and stir 1 minute. Add the chicken and stir-fry over low heat for 5 minutes, tossing to coat the meat with the spices. Add the balance of the stock, the lemongrass, rice vinegar, soy sauce, salt, and potato and combine well.

3.   Add the chili halves and tomato cubes and cook, covered, until the chicken is tender, about 20 minutes. The curry does not have a great deal of sauce. It does, however, have a substantial kick.

   Serve warm with rice.

SERVES 8 TO 10.

PANSOH AYAM
(ETHNIC PEOPLE, MANOK)

Chicken Roasted in Bamboo

The Dayak are the indigenous people of Borneo, specifically of Sarawak, where I was doing research for this book. The Iban are the sea Dayak or in past centuries the pirates who terrified the sea lanes. The Bidayuh were the land Dayak who were involved in agricultural pursuits. Now the Dayaks have been absorbed into the twentieth century and are Malaysians living in their *kampongs* (villages), but they are not homogenized. They still remember their traditions. For example, the Iban are weavers of cloth, while the Bidayuh weave mats and baskets. These explanations are in simple terms.

This recipe is of the Iban, with their soft gentle voices. I have included it for historical purposes.

1 *green bamboo cylinder, about 4 inches in diameter, 2 feet long*
  a 3-pound chicken, cut into pieces
1 *teaspoon salt*
1 *teaspoon pepper*
6 *cloves garlic, lightly smashed with the flat side of a cleaver*
2 *cups water*
  Banana leaves or aluminum foil

1. Prepare the bamboo cylinder for the chicken: The top should be open, the bottom node intact, thus sealing the bamboo.
2. Rub the chicken pieces with the salt, pepper, and garlic. Push the pieces of chicken and seasonings into the bamboo cylinder. Pour in the water, which should cover the chicken. Close off the top of the cylinder with folded banana leaves, or if not available use aluminum foil to seal the top.
3. Bake over charcoal for about ½ hour, turning the bamboo

cylinder now and then to cook the contents over a slow fire. When ready, remove the chicken and broth and serve them together.

Serve warm with rice.

SERVES 4 TO 6.

NOTE This method of cooking poultry or pork must be the earliest method of cooking food before clay or metal objects were invented for the kitchen. I have observed the entire process of preparing *pansoh* in Malaysia and Indonesia. The natural flavors of *kampong* chickens, with their stringy legs trained to race across village yards, were ideally rendered in the bamboo, which also tenderized the meat.

A cylinder of green bamboo, freshly cut, is the preferred kind, since there is enough moisture in the green wood to prevent it from not burning when placed over charcoal.

CHICKEN PONTEH (NONYA OF MALACCA)

Chicken with Brown Bean Paste

Nonya dishes have an enthusiastic following in Malaysia. Idiosyncratic combinations provide culinary interest, as we have in this chicken dish.

3   *shallots, sliced*
    a 1-inch piece ginger, sliced
5   *cloves garlic, sliced*
3   *tablespoons plus 2 cups water*
5   *tablespoons vegetable oil*
1   *teaspoon black soy sauce (*kicip *in Malay, see Glossary)*
1   *tablespoon ground brown bean paste (bottled)*
3   *pounds chicken parts, cut into 20 pieces, with or without bone*
½   *teaspoon salt*
1   *tablespoon sugar, or more to taste*
1   *potato, peeled and cut into 1-inch cubes (1 cup)*

1. Process the shallots, ginger, and garlic to a smooth paste with 3 tablespoons water.
2. Heat 3 tablespoons of the oil in a wok or large pan and stir-fry the spice paste over low heat until the aroma rises. Add the soy sauce, bean paste, and chicken and fry, turning it, for 5 minutes.
3. Add the 2 cups water, salt, and sugar and cook for 15 minutes.
4. In another skillet, pan fry the potato in the remaining 2 tablespoons oil until brown and softened, about 10 minutes. Add them to the chicken mixture and simmer, covered, over low heat until the ingredients are tender and the sauce, which is slightly sweet, has thickened.

    Serve warm with rice and side dishes.

SERVES 6 TO 8.

Manuk Lihing
(Ethnic People, Kadazan)

Chicken in Rice Wine

The Kadazan are the ethnic people living in the state of Sabah, Borneo. I went to one of their towns among the rural hills outside of Kota Kinabalu, noting their traditional houses raised on stilts. The Kadazan, now Christians, live close to nature and have a style of cooking that is simple and flavorful.

Their homemade sweet rice wine has a characteristic yeasty aroma that makes a very pleasant drink, but is also an inspired addition to this soup, which is celebrated for its strengthening qualities. Mothers are given the soup after the birth of a child to assist in a rapid recovery. Who can blame them!

   3   *pounds chicken parts, cut into 18 to 20 pieces*
 ½–1 *cup rice wine, depending on strength (see How to Make, page 296, and Note)*
   4   *cups boiling water*
   1   *teaspoon salt, or to taste*
       a 2-inch piece ginger, sliced thin
   2   *pieces wood ears (see Glossary), soaked in water 1 hour*
   1   *egg, beaten*

Put all the ingredients, except the egg, in a pan and bring to a boil. Stir in the egg. Simmer over low heat for about 45 minutes, long enough to prepare the soup and tenderize the chicken.

Serve warm.

SERVES 4 OR 5.

NOTE Commercial rice wine may be substituted.

Ayam Gulai (Ethnic People)

Chicken Curry from Sabah

Every case (read "region") is unique, and the taste of this chicken curry, which has similar ingredients to other curries, is no exception. Coconut milk, a few extra dried hot red chilis, and a thicker consistency provided by *kemiri* (macadamia nuts) make it distinct.

10	kemiri *(macadamia nuts), ground fine*
2	*medium onions, sliced (1 cup)*
5	*cloves garlic, sliced*
	a 2-inch piece ginger, sliced
5	*dried hot red chilis, broken up and boiled in $^1/_4$ cup water 1 minute*
2	*cups "regular" coconut milk (see page 14)*
	Vegetable oil
2	*stalks lemongrass, bottom 5 inches, cracked*
2	*kaffir lime leaves (available in Southeast Asian markets)*
$^1/_2$	*teaspoon turmeric*
1	*teaspoon salt*
$^1/_8$	*teaspoon pepper*
1	*tablespoon tamarind paste dissolved in $^1/_4$ cup water, strained (see How to Make, page 289)*
$^1/_2$	*cup water*
	a $3^1/_2$-pound chicken, cut into 12 pieces, loose skin and fat discarded

1. Process the *kemiri,* onions, garlic, ginger, chilis, and their soaking liquid with $^1/_2$ cup of the coconut milk to a smooth paste.
2. Heat the oil in a pan, and stir-fry the spice paste over low heat for 2 minutes. Add the lemongrass, lime leaves, turmeric, salt, pepper, balance of coconut milk, tamarind liquid, and water. Simmer for 5 minutes.
3. Add the chicken pieces, mix well, and simmer, covered, over

low heat for about ½ hour, or until the chicken is tender and the sauce has thickened.

Serve warm.

SERVES 6 WITH RICE AND SIDE DISHES.

Ayam Masak Kicip (Ethnic People)

Soy Sauce Chicken

The black soy sauce known as *kicip* is a paramount seasoning in a chicken dish from a Bidayuh *kampong* in Sarawak. The influence is Chinese. This flavor appeals to the indigenous people as more ingredients are added to what was, in the past, a simple form of cooking.

3	*cloves garlic, sliced*
	a 1-inch piece ginger, sliced
1/2	*teaspoon salt*
1/8	*teaspoon pepper*
3	*tablespoons water, plus more if needed*
3	*tablespoons vegetable oil*
1	*stalk lemongrass, bottom 5 inches, cracked*
2	*pounds chicken parts (10 pieces)*
3	*tablespoons black soy sauce (*kicip *in Malay, available in any Asian grocery)*
1	*teaspoon sugar*

1. Process the garlic, ginger, salt, and pepper to a paste with the water.
2. Heat the oil in a large pan, add the spice paste and lemongrass, and stir-fry over low heat until the aroma rises, about 3 minutes.
3. Add the chicken parts and brown them, turning them, for 5 minutes. Add the *kicip* and sugar and continue to fry until the chicken is tender, about 20 minutes. Should it require more time, add 1/4 cup water and fry, covered, until tender. There is no sauce; the chicken is coated with the seasonings.

    Serve warm with rice and mixed garden vegetables.

SERVES 4 OR 5.

NOTE The chicken was served with a platter of "veggie" from the *kampong* garden—longbeans, ferns, cassava, rice, all homegrown.

Ayam Masak Rebus (Ethnic People)

Chicken Stew from Padang Pan

One day at the *kampong* Padang Pan in Sarawak, I observed and was served this chicken stew. The young wife sent a boy out to catch one of her chickens. In a short while, the stew was cooking Bidayuh style.

3	*cloves garlic, sliced*
	a 1-inch piece ginger, sliced
1	*teaspoon salt*
¹⁄₈	*teaspoon pepper*
1¹⁄₂	*cups water*
2	*pounds chicken parts (10 pieces)*
1	*stalk lemongrass, bottom 5 inches, cracked*

1. Process the garlic, ginger, salt, and pepper with 3 tablespoons of the water to a paste.
2. Bring the balance of the water to a boil in a pan and add the paste, chicken, and lemongrass. Cover and simmer over low heat for about 35 minutes, or until the chicken is tender. There will be some sauce.

   Serve warm with rice and Ulam Ulam (page 156).

SERVES 4 TO 6.

KAMPONG PADANG PAN
SARAWAK

One day I traveled to the home of an ethnic friend, a Bidayuh, whose *kampong* is 1½ hours from a large town. Two vans with seating room for ten persons travel to the *kampong* once in the morning and afternoon. After the vans leave, there is no traffic over the dirt-and-loose-stone road, and we were forced to walk to a crossroad miles away to hitchhike to Kuching. We were picked up by a Chinese furniture manufacturer, who with great pleasure took us to my hotel. Then, to compound the extreme courtesy, he invited me to dinner at a seafood restaurant.

The Bidayuh's home (he commutes to his job in Kuching at the hotel I stayed in) was a sturdily constructed house with solid floors. Handwoven mats on the floor were woven by his father (and were for sale, as were the wonderfully constructed baskets woven by his mother). There was his wife, a homemaker, and three children.

The rains came during the day and never left. A great deluge of violent water immersed the land for hours at a time. It was the monsoon. Then it cleared up. Everything grew with abandon during the monsoon season.

A mountainside of pepper vines and cassava plants were all over the place. Red sweet potatoes, pineapples, bananas, ducks, chickens, cacao trees, and mango grew in profusion.

Lo A (Nonya)
Braised Duck with Kicip

Duck recipes are hard to come by in Malaysia, since Malays and Indians do not eat duck, which is considered a preoccupation of the Chinese. But the Nonya are people of Chinese ancestry, so this recipe fits into that category.

Kicip is a thick, black soy sauce and is reminiscent of the Indonesian *kecap*—sweetened seasoned soy sauce. *Kicip* is always purchased and never made in the home.

¼   *cup corn oil*
2   *large onions, sliced (1½ cups)*
    a 2-inch piece galangal (see Glossary), cracked
4   *whole star anise*
4   *whole cloves*
1   *teaspoon black or white pepper*
1   *whole duck, 4–4½ pounds, loose skin and fat discarded*
2   *tablespoons* kicip *(see above)*
4   *cups water*
½   *teaspoon salt*
1   *tablespoon sugar*
    a 3-inch piece cinnamon stick

1. Heat the oil in a large pan, add the onions, galangal, star anise, cloves, and pepper, and stir-fry over low heat for 5 minutes, until the onions become golden brown.

2. Add the whole duck and stir to coat it all over with the seasonings, about 10 minutes. Add the *kicip*, water, salt, sugar, and cinnamon stick, cover the pan, and simmer over low heat until the duck is tender, about 1 hour. Turn the duck over now and then while it cooks in the broth. Remove the duck and carve it into not-too-large serving pieces, about 3 inches each. Strain the cooking liquid and serve as a gravy.

    Serve warm.

SERVES 8 WITH THE DUCK GRAVY AND WHITE RICE.

Serati Sorai (Ethnic People)

Kampong Duck with Lemongrass

Not too far from a *kampong* in the interior of Sarawak, while I was visiting a friend I was sitting near a wide stream that was a little muddy from the the monsoon rains but still flowing smoothly. A few hundred yards upstream a water buffalo and her calf splashed in the river, then raced on to the shore. A log floated downstream, aquatic birds swam within my view. Across the river, a Bidayuh woman was tending her garden. The silence was expressive.

Suddenly, the log moved with a thrash of its tail and a duck disappeared with a startled squawk. A few feathers floated on the water. The log sank, then appeared again and moved slowly toward the sea.

5   *shallots, sliced*
2   *cloves garlic, sliced*
    a 2-inch piece ginger, sliced
3   *cups water*
2   *tablespoons corn oil*
1   *stalk lemongrass, bottom 5 inches, cracked*
1   *duck (about 4¹/₂ pounds), cut into 12 pieces, fat and loose skin discarded*
2   *whole star anise*
2   *whole cloves*
    a 3-inch piece stick cinnamon
2   *cardamom pods*
1   *tablespoon black soy sauce (* kicip *in Malay, see Glossary)*
1   *teaspoon sugar*

1. Process the shallots, garlic, and ginger with ¹/₄ cup of the water to a smooth paste.
2. Heat the oil in a pan, add the spice paste and lemongrass, and stir-fry over low heat for 3 minutes as the aroma rises.
3. Add the duck pieces, star anise, cloves, cinnamon stick, and cardamom pods and fry for 5 minutes to brown the duck lightly.

Add the balance of the water, soy sauce, and sugar, and bring to a boil. Cover the pan and simmer for 1 hour, or until the duck is tender. If the liquid evaporates too quickly, add another ¼ cup water. There is some sauce, enough to keep the duck moist.

Serve warm with rice.

SERVES 8.

ITIK MASAK BEREMPAH (ETHNIC PEOPLE)

Aromatic Roast Duck

Nothing pleases me more than a new duck recipe and the home-maker who can cook it to perfection within the framework of her tra-ditions. That is what happened in this case with a local Iban recipe in Sarawak. The name of the recipe could also be "Twice-Cooked Duck," since it is first boiled with an assortment of spices, then oven-roasted. Any homecook can do it.

1	*whole clove*
4	*cardamom pods*
1	*star anise*
	a 2-inch piece cinnamon stick
1	*teaspoon salt*
$^1/_8$	*teaspoon pepper*
2	*cloves garlic, sliced*
2	*shallots, sliced*
	a 1-inch piece ginger, sliced
5	*cups water*
1	*whole duck (4¹/₂ pounds), loose skin and fat discarded*
1	*tablespoon honey*
	Fresh coriander, for garnish

1. Process the clove, cardamom, star anise, cinnamon, salt, pep-per, garlic, shallots, and ginger to a relatively smooth paste us-ing ¹/₃ cup of the water to moisten the paste.
2. Put the duck in a large pan with the balance of the water. Bring to a boil and add the spice paste. Cook at a simmer, cov-ered, over low heat for 1 hour, basting now and then. This should be enough time to tenderize the duck almost to com-pletion.
3. Remove the duck and hang it or let it air-dry it for 1 to 2 hours. Then, paint the duck with all of the honey. Put the duck in a

roasting pan and bake in a preheated 325-degree oven for ½ hour to brown and crisp the skin.

4. Reserve the pan gravy and combine it with 1 cup of the spice paste. Since ducks are fat, my suggestion is to put the spice sauce in a small bowl and put it in the freezer for ½ hour. The fat will congeal on the top and can then be discarded. Reheat the spiced sauce.

5. Cut the duck into about 16 serving pieces. Put them on a serving platter and pour the *hot* fat-free sauce over the pieces. Garnish generously with sprigs of fresh coriander.

Serve warm with rice and side dishes.

SERVES 8.

ITIK SOLO (MALAY)

Barbecued Duck

It was mid-November, the height of the monsoon rains that pelted Kota Bahru in Kelantan state with particular intensity. It had rained for three days and nights with an occasional break in the weather. Our van was en route to the Sultan's lady cook who was going to demonstrate several sweets for me. Upon entering the muddy court-yard, we observed several ducks waddling in the mud and rain. This was very auspicious for me since neither Malays nor Indians eat duck, which is considered a monopoly of the Chinese. Duck recipes, not surprisingly, are difficult to find in Malaysia. Here is a recipe fit for the Sultan's table.

	a 4¹/₂-pound duck
6	*cups water*
1	*teaspoon salt*
6	*shallots, sliced*
	a 1-inch piece ginger, sliced
¹/₄	*teaspoon curry powder*
¹/₂	*teaspoon hot red chili powder*
¹/₄	*teaspoon sugar*
2	*teaspoons tamarind paste dissolved in ¹/₄ cup water, strained (see How to Make, page 289)*
	a ¹/₂-inch piece galangal (see Glossary), sliced
¹/₄	*teaspoon fenugreek seed (halba in Malay)*
2	*cups "regular" coconut milk (see page 14)*
1	*stalk lemongrass, bottom 5 inches, cracked*

1. Put the duck in a large pan, add the water and salt, and bring the water to a boil. Cover the pan and cook over low heat for 1 hour, enough to tenderize the duck. Drain, which will eliminate significant amounts of fat.

2. Process the shallots, ginger, curry powder, chili powder, sugar,

tamarind liquid, galangal, and fenugreek seed to a smooth paste with ½ cup of the coconut milk in a blender. Transfer to a pan, add the balance of the coconut milk and lemongrass, and simmer over low heat for 15 minutes, which will thicken the sauce.

3. Put the duck in a roasting pan, cover it with the spice paste, and roast in a preheated 400-degree oven for 20 minutes, basting once or twice during this time.

Another way to cook the duck is to put it rubbed with the spice paste in a pan and barbecue it in a gas or electric oven broiler for 15 minutes.

In the lady cook's kitchen, the duck was speared on a long metal skewer, rubbed inside and out with the spice paste, and barbecued over a fire of charcoal and coconut husks. This traditional method also lightly smokes the duck as it crisps the skin.

Serve warm with rice and side dishes.

SERVES 6 OR 7.

Modern mosque in Kuantan.

BEEF, MUTTON, AND OTHER MEATS

The heavy meats—beef, mutton, and pork—are the difficult ones in the tropical heat of Malaysia. That said, beef and mutton (lamb) dishes are predominantly popular in the Malay community, although both Chinese and Muslim Indians also use these meats. Pork has a certain popularity, without religious restriction, among the Chinese and Ethnic People of Borneo.

The great classic beef dish is Rendang (page 90). Its heavily spiced, substantial texture is usually enjoyed in small quantities since one could not attack a plate of this and consume it without weighing its heaviness. But it would always be prepared for celebrations and special events as a traditional and expected addition to the menu.

In the temperate climate of North America the meat dishes of Malaysia, with their catalogue of spices, should find a willing audience quite easily.

RENDANG (MALAY)

Slow-Cook Spiced Beef

Rendang, a most popular dish, must be heavily seasoned, cooked slowly and dry, without sauce, to be correctly made. It is a favorite during Ramadan and other celebratory occasions. The beef is cooked with ginger, galangal, hot chilis, palm sugar, among other seasonings, over low heat in a covered wok or pan until almost tender. Then the meat cubes are saturated with coconut milk and cooked some more.

The preparation of *rendang* vividly illustrates the lengths the Malaysians will go to prepare their traditional foods with a host of ingredients. The Indonesians also prepare beef *rendang*, but with a different number of ingredients.

 3   *shallots, sliced, or 1 medium onion, sliced (¹/₂ cup)*
 3   *stalks lemongrass, root end bulb only, trimmed, sliced thin*
 2   *cloves garlic, sliced*
     a ¹/₂-inch piece ginger, sliced
 2   *slices galangal (see Glossary)*
 1   *tablespoon tamarind paste dissolved in 3 tablespoons water, strained (see How to Make, page 289)*
¹/₄ *teaspoon turmeric*
5–6 *dried hot red chilis, to taste, soaked in ¹/₂ cup water*
 2   *tablespoons palm sugar (gula Malacca, see Glossary) or brown sugar*
1¹/₂ *pounds boneless beef chuck or rump steak, cut into 1-inch cubes*
 1   *cup "regular" coconut milk (see page 14)*
 2   *fresh kaffir lime leaves (available in Southeast Asian markets), sliced thin*
¹/₄ *cup grated unsweetened dessicated coconut, toasted (kerisik, page 91)*

1. Process the shallots, lemongrass, garlic, ginger, galangal, tamarind liquid, turmeric, chilis and soaking water, and sugar to a relatively smooth paste.

2. Put the paste in a wok or large pan with the beef and cook, covered, over low heat until almost tender, stirring frequently, about 1 hour.

3. Add the coconut milk, lime leaves, and *kerisik* (see Note) and combine well. Cover the pan and cook until the beef is tender and all the sauce has evaporated. *(Rendang* is a dry preparation and will take about 1½ hours to cook over low heat. There are those who prefer the beef cubes to be quite dry and tender and others who prefer it with a slight amount of moisture.)

Serve warm or room temperature.

SERVES 6.

NOTE *Kerisik,* puréed toasted coconut, is an important ingredient when preparing Rendang.

½ *cup grated unsweetened dessicated coconut*
1 *teaspoon vegetable oil*

1. Toast the coconut in a nonstick skillet over low heat for about 10 minutes to brown.

2. Put the coconut in a blender with the oil and process to a smooth oily paste. Use in *rendang* or other dishes where *kerisik* is called for.

RENDANG DAGING TOK PERAK (MALAY)

Grandfather's Spiced Beef Superior

There are a variety of *rendangs*—essentially slow-cooked beef cubes heavily spiced and flavored with coconut milk and toasted coconut shreds *(kerisik)*. This recipe is intensely flavored, too, but is different from beef preparations in other regions. It is from the home of a favorite chef's grandfather. The *rendang* in that family is always known as grandfather's since he liked the assortment of spices and seasonings. Personal preference is the guide here.

1   *cup grated unsweetened dessicated coconut mixed with 1 teaspoon
    vegetable oil*
2   *pounds boneless beef chuck, cut into $^1/_2$-inch cubes*
6   *shallots, sliced thin*
    a 2-inch piece ginger, peeled and sliced thin
3   *stalks lemongrass, bottom 5 inches, cracked*
3   *kaffir lime leaves (available in Southeast Asian markets)*
    a 1-inch piece galangal (see Glossary), peeled and sliced thin
$^1/_4$ *teaspoon turmeric*
1   *teaspoon hot red chili powder*
$^1/_2$ *teaspoon ground cumin*
$^1/_2$ *teaspoon curry powder*
$^1/_2$ *teaspoon ground fennel*
$^1/_2$ *teaspoon ground cinnamon*
$^1/_4$ *teaspoon ground cardamom*
3   *lobes star anise*
$^1/_4$ *teaspoon salt*
$^1/_4$ *cup palm sugar* (gula Malacca, *see Glossary and Note below*)
1   *cup "regular" coconut milk (see page 14)*

1. Put the grated coconut in a nonstick pan and stir-fry continuously over low heat until the shreds turn brown. Set aside.
2. Put the beef and all the remaining ingredients, except the

toasted coconut, in a large pan and stir-fry over low heat for 5 minutes. Then cook for 1 hour, stirring frequently. (There is very little liquid and one has to keep the heat low and the wooden spoon stirring.)

3.   When the beef is tender but still moist, add the reserved toasted coconut and stir-fry another 5 minutes to integrate the mixture.

This is a concentrated beef dish and one cannot eat more than 2 or 3 cubes of meat in a menu that includes rice, a vegetable stir fry, and a chili-hot side dish.

SERVES 8.

NOTE *Gula Malacca* has a richly endowed flavor that is more intense than brown cane sugar, but that may be substituted if all else fails.

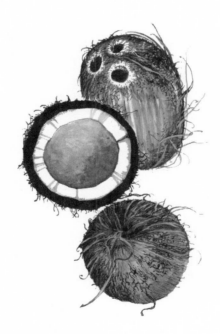

Masak Daging Merah (Malay)

Red Beef

Malaysia is not a dairy country. It is much too hot. For reasons of expediency, canned evaporated milk has crept into the cuisine, and the Malays, Indians, and Chinese all use it. In this recipe the choice is extended to yogurt, which is closer to the original taste in India.

2–3 *tablespoons hot red chili powder, to taste*
2 *medium onions, sliced (1 cup)*
2 *cloves garlic, sliced*
a ¹/₂-inch piece ginger, sliced
¹/₄ *cup water*
2 *tablespoons corn oil*
3 *cardamom pods*
3 *whole cloves*
a 3-inch piece cinnamon stick
1 *whole star anise*
2 *stalks lemongrass, bottom 5 inches, cracked*
1 *tablespoon tomato ketchup*
1 *tablespoon bottled chili sauce*
2 *pounds boneless beef chuck, sliced into 2-inch pieces ¹/₄ inch thick*
1 *tablespoon tamarind paste dissolved in 3 tablespoons water, strained (see How to Make, page 289)*
1 *teaspoon sugar*
¹/₂ *teaspoon salt*
¹/₂ *cup evaporated milk or plain yogurt*

1. Process the chili powder, onions, garlic, and ginger with the water to a relatively smooth paste.
2. Heat the oil in a large pan, add the cardamom pods, cloves, cinnamon stick, and star anise (these four spices are known as the *rempah*) and stir-fry over low heat for ¹/₂ minute. Add the onion

paste and lemongrass and stir-fry for 3 minutes to create a spice aroma.

3.   Add the tomato ketchup, chili sauce, and beef and stir-fry for 4 minutes. Stir in the tamarind liquid, sugar, and salt and stir to combine well. Add the evaporated milk or yogurt and continue to cook the thinly sliced meat until tender, about 30 to 40 minutes, and integrated with the small amount of sauce.

Serve warm with rice or bread.

SERVES 8 WITH OTHER DISHES.

Rampah Kerutup (Malay)

Spiced Ramadan Beef

My cooking teacher told me that in his home *rampah kerutup* was served in the evenings of Ramadan when it was permissible to eat. The dish is a catalogue of the seasonings of Kelantan, where a variety of spices results in an unusually satisfying preparation for a celebration.

2 *cups shredded fresh or unsweetened dessicated coconut*
1 *tablespoon tamarind paste dissolved in 3 tablespoons water, strained (see How to Make, page 289)*
¼ *cup chopped fresh coriander*
2 *teaspoons ground cumin*
2 *teaspoons ground fennel*
  a 2-inch piece galangal (see Glossary), sliced
¼ *teaspoon turmeric*
2 *hot red dried chilis, broken up*
5 *shallots, sliced*
3 *cloves garlic, sliced*
  a ½-inch piece ginger, sliced
½ *teaspoon* belacan, *toasted (see Glossary)*
2 *cups "regular" coconut milk (see page 14)*
1 *tablespoon corn oil*
2 *pounds boneless beef chuck, cut into 1-inch cubes*
½ *teaspoon salt, or to taste*

1. Toast the coconut shreds in a nonstick pan over low heat for about 5 minutes without oil until brown, stirring constantly to avoid burning. Set aside.
2. Process the tamarind liquid, coriander, cumin, fennel, galangal, turmeric, chilis, shallots, garlic, ginger, and *belacan* with ½ cup of the coconut milk to a smooth paste.
3. Heat the oil in a large pan, add the spice paste, toasted shred-

ded coconut, and beef. Stir-fry over low heat for 5 minutes as the color of the beef changes. Add the balance of the coconut milk and salt, bring to a boil, and cook, covered, over low heat until the beef is tender, about 45 minutes.

Serve with bread, rice, or Roti Canai (page 24).

SERVES 8.

Satay (all Malaysia)

The Barbecue

Everyone likes satay, the preeminent Malaysian (and Indonesian) barbecue presented on slim rounded 6-inch bamboo skewers. Boneless beef or chicken are the meats of choice, although it is possible to include lamb, or even shrimp, which is less frequent. Fish is not recommended.

There are two steps in the preparation of satay. The first is to marinate the meat in a well-seasoned marinade with traditional spices at room temperature for four hours. Four pieces of meat are then skewered, ready for barbecuing over charcoal. Gas or electric tabletop broilers are available in this part of the world and are workable, but charcoal is the most natural and flavorful method. Gas or electric oven broilers are also acceptable.

1	*pound beef steak or chicken breast*
1	*small onion, sliced (1/3 cup)*
4	*cloves garlic, sliced*
2	*stalks lemongrass, root end bulb only, trimmed, sliced thin*
	a 1/2-inch piece galangal (see Glossary), sliced
1/2	*teaspoon turmeric*
1	*teaspoon ground coriander*
1/2	*teaspoon ground cumin*
1/2	*teaspoon ground fennel*
1	*teaspoon salt*
2	*tablespoons white or brown sugar*
2	*tablespoons tamarind paste dissolved in 1/4 cup water, strained (see How to Make, page 289)*
30	*wooden skewers*
	vegetable oil for the skewers
	Warm Peanut Sauce (recipe follows)

1. Trim the beef or chicken and cut into 3/4-inch cubes.
2. Process the onion, garlic, lemongrass, galangal, turmeric, co-

riander, cumin, fennel, salt, sugar, and tamarind liquid into a relatively smooth paste.

3. Mix the spice paste with the meat and marinate for 4 hours at room temperature or longer if refrigerated.

4. Assemble the satays: Rub the skewers with oil and thread 4 pieces of meat on the pointed end of each skewer. Make certain that the meat covers the skewer from the first cube to the last, pressing them flat and close together. Should the skewer show through it might burn during cooking. The satays are ready for cooking. Set aside.

5. When ready to cook: Barbecue the skewers over charcoal, turning them, for 2 minutes on each side.

Serve warm with the warm peanut sauce.

MAKES ABOUT 30 SKEWERS.

WARM PEANUT SAUCE

Satay sauce is one of the finest sauces in all of Asia and one that is copied here and there but never excelled. It is based on coarsely crushed peanuts superbly enveloped by Malaysian seasonings such as galangal, tamarind liquid, lemongrass, and especially hot red dried chilis, which are added according to personal preference.

1   *tablespoon hot red chili powder, or more to taste*
1   *medium onion, sliced*
2   *cloves garlic, sliced*
2   *stalks lemongrass, root bulb only, sliced thin*
    a ¹/₂-inch piece galangal (see Glossary), sliced
¹/₄ *teaspoon* petis udang *(shrimp paste), optional but recommended, see Glossary*
1   *cup water*
3   *tablespoons corn oil*
2   *cups roasted peanuts, coarsely ground*
2   *tablespoons tamarind paste dissolved in 2 tablespoons water, strained (see How to Make, page 289)*
2   *tablespoons brown sugar*
¹/₄ *teaspoon salt*

1.   Process the chili powder, onion, garlic, lemongrass, galangal, and shrimp paste, if using, until fairly smooth. Add 2 of the tablespoons water to moisten as you process.

2.   Warm the oil in a pan and fry the spice paste over low heat for about 10 minutes. Add the peanuts, tamarind liquid, and the balance of the water and bring the sauce to simmer. Add the sugar and salt and cook until the sauce thickens, about 15 minutes. Adjust the sugar and chili powder. Keep the sauce warm.

   Should the sauce become too thick, add several tablespoons water.

MAKES ABOUT 3 CUPS PEANUT SAUCE.

SATAY DIP (CHINESE)

This extraordinary combination is a specialty of Ipoh, a predominantly Chinese culinary city known by many as a "food paradise." This dip can be served with chicken, beef, or lamb satays, with equal enthusiasm. Untraditional but certainly effective is to use the dip with blanched vegetables, such as string beans, cauliflower, red or green peppers, and the inevitable carrot.

3   *shallots, sliced*
2   *cloves garlic, sliced*
    a ¹/₂-inch piece ginger, sliced
¹/₄ *cup water*
1   *inch lemongrass (from root end)*
1   *tablespoon vegetable oil*
¹/₂ *cup mashed potato*
2   *teaspoons hot red chili powder*
¹/₂ *cup "regular" coconut milk (see page 14)*
³/₄ *cup coarsely chopped roasted peanuts*
1   *tablespoon sugar*
1   *teaspoon salt*

Process the shallots, garlic, ginger, and water to a paste. Put the paste in a pan with the remaining ingredients, bring to a boil, and simmer over low heat for 10 minutes. Adjust sugar and salt to your taste if necessary.

Serve at room temperature with any kind of satays. Do not refrigerate.

MAKES ABOUT 2 CUPS.

VARIATION Some cooks to replace the potato with boiled mashed pumpkin. Or, you can also use ¹/₂ cup mashed white potato and ¹/₄ cup mashed pumpkin.

Kambing Kurma (Malay)

Lamb Chops in Spice Sauce

Kurma, according to a dictionary definition, is "a spiced dish" and that is what this delectable lamb is all about. Of particular interest is the *rempah,* the four spices that are also known as the four brothers. Added at the same time to the pan, they are star anise, cinnamon stick, cardamom pod, and whole clove, and they transform this *kurma* into much more than an ordinary spiced dish.

2	*tablespoons corn oil*
4	*shallots, sliced*
3	*cloves garlic, sliced*
	a 1-inch piece ginger, sliced
1	*tablespoon ground coriander seed*
1	*tablespoon ground fennel*
1	*tablespoon ground cumin*
1	*cup water*
2	*pounds rib or shoulder lamb chops, cut into 3 inch pieces*
2	*stalks lemongrass, bottom 5 inches, cracked*
1	*whole star anise*
	a 1-inch piece cinnamon stick
3	*cardamom pods*
2	*whole cloves*
¹/₂	*cup plain yogurt*
5	kemiri *(macadamia nuts)*
1	*teaspoon salt, or to taste*
¹/₈	*teaspoon pepper*

1. Heat the oil in a large pan. Add the shallots, garlic, and ginger and sauté over low heat until golden. Combine the coriander, fennel, cumin, and ¹/₃ cup of the water and stir it into the mixture.

2. Add the lamb, lemongrass, star anise, cinnamon stick, car-

damom pods, and cloves and sauté over low heat for 5 minutes. Stir in the yogurt, *kemiri*, the balance of the water, salt, and pepper.

3. Cover the pan and simmer for 20 minutes. Test the lamb for tenderness. If necessary, cook a little longer. There should be little sauce at the end of the cooking time.

    Serve warm with rice.

SERVES 8.

SATAY KAMBING (MALAY)

Barbecued Mutton Satays

Probably the most popular street food, found everywhere, and with a variety of flavors depending upon the region, satays can be made with mutton, chicken, or beef steak. Mutton, old English colonial usage, is, of course, another word for lamb. Regardless of which meat you prefer, it is the peanut sauce that defines the ultimate taste of a satay, and on this rests the success of any satay.

The Mutton

4   *cloves garlic, sliced*
2   *hearts of lemongrass, 3 inches of root end, sliced thin*
1/2 *teaspoon salt*
1/2 *teaspoon pepper*
1/2 *teaspoon turmeric*
2   *tablespoons water*
2   *pounds boneless lamb, cut into pieces 1 inch long and 1/4 inch thick*

The Peanut Sauce

1   *tablespoon corn oil*
4   *shallots, sliced*
3   *cloves garlic, sliced*
3–4 *tablespoons* chili boh *(see How to Make, page 290)*
1   *cup water*
1   *stalk lemongrass, bottom 5 inches, cracked*
1   *tablespoon tamarind paste dissolved in 3 tablespoons water, strained (see How to Make, page 289)*
1/2 *teaspoon salt*
1   *tablespoon brown sugar, or more to taste*
     a 1-inch piece galangal (see Glossary), cracked
2/3 *cup roasted peanuts, coarsely chopped*
30   *wooden skewers, soaked in water 1 hour to prevent burning*

1. Prepare the mutton: Process the garlic, lemongrass, salt, pepper, turmeric, and the water to a smooth paste. Add the lamb and marinate for 1 to 2 hours at room temperature.
2. Prepare the sauce: Heat the oil in a pan. Add the shallots, garlic, and chili paste and stir-fry over low heat for 2 minutes.
3. Add the water, lemongrass, tamarind liquid, salt, brown sugar, and galangal and bring to a boil. Simmer over low heat for 10 minutes. Stir in the peanuts, mix well, and remove from the heat. Keep warm.
4. Prepare the satays: Thread 4 pieces of lamb onto each skewer, pushing the pieces close together. Barbecue, turning them, over charcoal or under a gas or electric broiler for 3 to 4 minutes. (Charcoal is better.)

    Serve with generous slices of unpeeled young cucumber and warm peanut sauce.

MAKES 30 SATAYS.

DAGING KICIP (INDIAN MUSLIM)

Sweet Spiced Beef

A friend in a tiny Indian Muslim restaurant, unexpected in Kuching, Sarawak, produced a local dish: lightly spiced beef cubes with hot chili. The basis of the flavor rested on the aromatic spices of star anise, cardamom, clove, and cinnamon, and a generous amount of *kicip* —dark thick soy sauce.

4   *cloves garlic, sliced*
    a 1-inch piece ginger, sliced
1   *tablespoon plus 1–1½ cups water*
2   *pounds boneless beef chuck, cut into ½-inch cubes*
1   *whole star anise*
2   *cardamom pods*
    a 1-inch piece cinnamon stick
2   *whole cloves*
¼   *teaspoon pepper*
2   *tablespoons vegetable oil*
1   *medium onion, sliced (½ cup)*
¼   *teaspoon turmeric*
½   *teaspoon hot red chili powder*
1   *tablespoon tomato paste*
3   *tablespoons black soy sauce (*kicip *in Malay, see Glossary)*
1   *teaspoon sugar*
    lemon wedges for serving

1. Process the garlic and ginger to a smooth paste with the 1 tablespoon water. Set aside.
2. Heat a skillet *without oil.* Add the beef cubes, star anise, cardamom pods, cinnamon stick, cloves, and pepper and stir-fry over low heat for 4 minutes.
3. Add the oil, onion, garlic/ginger paste, turmeric, chili powder, tomato paste, soy sauce, and sugar and mix well for 2 minutes.

4. Add the 1 cup water, bring to a boil, and simmer over low heat for about 45 minutes, or until the beef is tender. Should the liquid evaporate, add another ½ cup water. There is some dark sauce for the beef.

    Serve warm, with the lemon wedges, and rice.

SERVES 8.

ADU MASALA (INDIAN)

Dry Mutton Curry

No one in Malaysia uses the term "lamb." "Mutton" is the preferred name, which also implies that the animal had a certain age. No matter, this lamb curry is traditional and moist, but does not have a sauce.

3 *tablespoons corn oil*
   a 2-inch piece cinnamon stick
3 *cardamom pods*
3 *whole cloves*
2 *whole star anise*
2 *medium onions, sliced thin (1 cup)*
   a 1/2-inch piece ginger, chopped
2 *cloves garlic, chopped*
2 *pounds boneless lamb, cut into 1/2-inch cubes*
1 *teaspoon salt, or to taste*
2 *cups water*
1 *tablespoon chili powder, or more or less, to taste*
3 *teaspoons ground cumin*
2 *teaspoons ground coriander*
1 *teaspoon ground fennel*
1/2 *teaspoon turmeric*
2 *teaspoons ground poppy seed (khus khus)*
1 *cup fresh or frozen green peas, blanched in hot water 2 minutes*

1. Heat the oil in a pan and add the cinnamon stick, cardamom pods, cloves, and star anise over moderate heat. When sizzling, after a moment, add the onions and stir-fry until golden brown. Add the ginger and garlic and mix well.
2. Add the lamb cubes and stir-fry them 1 minute. Add the salt and water, bring to a boil, and simmer over low heat for about 45 minutes.

3. Add the chili powder, cumin, coriander, fennel, turmeric, and ground poppy seeds and cook for 15 minutes, until reduced to a moist curry but without any sauce. The meat should be tender. At the last minute, just before serving, fold in the green peas.

Serve warm with rice.

SERVE 8 TO 10.

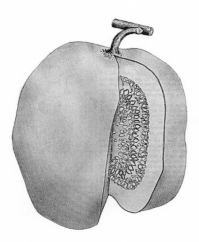

Jani Masak Halia (Ethnic People)

Pork with Ginger

Unlike the Muslims, who do not eat pork at all, the indigenous people of Sarawak do not have any restrictions regarding meat. Pork, therefore, is an important food. In recent years for the Iban and Bidayuh there has been an acceptance of Chinese flavors and cooking techniques. This pork dish has a very strong Chinese influence.

2	*pounds boneless pork, fat and skin trimmed, sliced into 2-inch thin pieces*
1	*egg, beaten*
2	*tablespoons flour*
	oil for deep frying
	a 1-inch piece ginger, sliced into julienne strips
2	*cloves garlic, smashed with the flat side of a cleaver*
1	*medium onion, halved and sliced*
1	*fresh hot red chili, seeded and sliced into julienne strips*
1	*tablespoon oyster sauce*
1/3	*cup water*
1/4	*teaspoon salt*
1/8	*teaspoon pepper*
2	*scallions, sliced into 2-inch lengths, then cut into julienne strips*

1. Put the pork slices in a bowl, add the egg, and mix well. Add the flour and combine well.

2. Heat enough oil for deep frying in a wok and fry the pork over moderate heat for 1 minute. Remove the pork with a slotted spoon to a metal strainer and set aside.

3. Remove all the oil except 1 tablespoon from the wok. Add the ginger, garlic, and onion and stir-fry for 1 minute over moderate heat. Add the pork slices and toss to combine. Now add the chili, oyster sauce, water, salt, and pepper, bring to a simmer,

and simmer the mixture over low heat for 3 minutes. Stir in the scallions.

Serve warm with rice and salads.

SERVES 8 TO 10.

STIR FRIED BEEF WITH CHAP CHOY (CHINESE)

Chap choy are assorted vegetables that can be included in a stir-fry according to personal preference. I suggest cauliflower florets, carrots sliced on the diagonal, celery slices, red or green sweet peppers, snow peas, or broccoli florets. A mixture of several is colorful, but one may prefer to use all of them in small quantities.

1   *pound flank steak or other beef steak, cut into 2-inch slices*
1   *tablespoon vegetable oil*
2   *slices ginger*
2   *cloves garlic, smashed with the flat side of a cleaver*
2   *cups fresh vegetables of choice (see above)*
1/3 *cup sliced canned bamboo shoots, rinsed and drained*
1/2 *teaspoon salt*
1/8 *teaspoon pepper*
1/4 *cup chicken broth*
1   *fresh hot red chili, seeded and sliced into julienne strips*
1   *scallion, sliced*

1.   Heat the oil in a wok or large skillet, add the beef slices, and stir-fry over moderate heat for 2 minutes. Set aside.
2.   In the same oil, stir-fry the ginger a moment. Add the garlic, beef, mixed vegetables, and bamboo shoots and stir-fry over moderate heat for 2 minutes.
3.   Add the salt, pepper, and chicken broth and stir-fry for 2 minutes. Stir in the chili and scallion and remove from the heat.
     Serve warm with rice.

SERVES 6 WITH OTHER DISHES.

SEAFOOD

Malaysia is surrounded by the South China Sea and its fish-filled waters. It follows that the Malaysian diet is predominantly from the sea. Fish is available and plentiful, and the buyer has the added incentive of it being economical. The standard fish purchase is direct: from the fishing boat to the cook in the kitchen, unlike other places where frozen fish and seafood is the norm.

Fortunately, the culinary fastidiousness of the Malaysian communities and their traditional cooking has elevated eating to dining. Even the simple barbecues, with few seasoning ingredients, are enriched with fresh seafood, herbs, and spices.

Of course, the ubiquitous hot chili, both green and red, fresh or

Big fish from the South China Sea.

dried, asserts its flavor and sting in various degrees in the curries lavishly seasoned with galangal, coconut milk, tamarind liquid, lemon leaves, ginger, garlic, turmeric, lemongrass, cinnamon, star anise, cardamom, and cloves, among other exotic ingredients. The list is long. How can one not be intrigued and ultimately enticed by recipes for both fish and shellfish that reveal the glories of traditional ethnic cooking from a remarkable part of the world?

Ikan Tongkol Gulai (Malay)

Tuna Fish Curry

Tuna and mackerel are both oily dark-fleshed fish and lend themselves to this curry, which is served for a traditional Kelantan breakfast with Nasi Dagang #1 (page 14).

3–4   *small fresh hot red chilis, sliced and seeded*
  4   *shallots, sliced*
      a ¹/₂-inch piece galangal (see Glossary), sliced
      a ¹/₂-inch piece ginger, sliced
  1   *teaspoon curry powder*
 ¹/₂   *teaspoon salt, or to taste*
 ¹/₂   *teaspoon sugar*
  1   *teaspoon turmeric*
  1   *tablespoon tamarind paste dissolved in ¹/₄ cup water, strained (see How
      to Make, page 289)*
  2   *cups "regular" coconut milk (see page 14)*
  1   *pound tuna or mackerel fillet, cut into 2-inch cubes*

1. Process the chilis, shallots, galangal, ginger, curry powder, salt,
   sugar, turmeric, and tamarind liquid with ¹/₂ cup of the coconut
   milk to a smooth paste.
2. Put the paste and balance of the coconut milk in a pan, bring to
   a boil, and simmer over low heat for 10 minutes.
3. Add the tuna or mackerel and simmer for 20 more minutes.
   Serve warm with rice.

SERVES 6.

GULAI IKAN (MALAY)

Fish Curry for the Nasi Dagang

A *gulai* is a curry cooked in Malay style. With its idiosyncratic ingredients and emphasis on hot red dried chilis and coconut milk, it is not for the timid. It is, however, remarkably flavorful and an outstanding method of cooking tuna, which abound in the waters of the South China Sea.

The Tuna

3   *cups water*
1   *teaspoon salt, or to taste*
2   *tablespoons tamarind paste dissolved in ¹/₂ cup water, strained (see How to Make, page 289)*
2   *pounds fresh tuna, sliced 1 inch thick*

The Sauce

1   *tablespoon ground coriander seed*
1   *teaspoon ground fennel*
    a 1¹/₂-inch piece galangal (see Glossary), sliced
3   *medium onions, sliced (1¹/₂ cups)*
7–10 *hot red dried chilis, to taste*
4   *cups "regular" coconut milk (see page 14)*

1. Prepare the tuna: Bring the water and salt to a boil and add the tamarind liquid and tuna. Cover the pan and simmer over low heat for about 20 minutes, until almost all the liquid is evaporated. Set aside.
2. Prepare the sauce: Process the coriander seed, fennel, galangal, onions, and chilis with ¹/₂ cup of the coconut milk to a smooth paste.

3. Bring the balance of the coconut milk to a boil over low heat. Add the spice paste and simmer, uncovered, over low heat for 15 minutes.

4. Add the tuna and whatever remains of the liquid in the pan to the sauce, simmer for 3 minutes, and serve immediately.

SERVES 8 WITH RICE.

VARIATION An equal amount of large mackerel may be used instead of the more expensive fresh tuna.

KARI KEPALA IKAN (MALAY)

Fish Head Curry

What makes this curry so popular? The Chinese and Malays, especially, respect the head of a fish, the larger the better, with its hidden morsels of sweet meat lurking among the flotsam and jetsam of the head bones. This recipe elevates the lowly head of a fish to something approaching a miraculous transformation, with a catalogue of spices and seasonings bound together with coconut milk.

4   *shallots, sliced*
    a 1-inch piece ginger, sliced
2   *cloves garlic, sliced*
2   *cups "regular" coconut milk (see page 14)*
2   *tablespoons corn oil*
    a 1-inch piece cinnamon stick
1   *whole star anise*
3   *cardamom pods*
2   *whole cloves*
2   *tablespoons curry powder*
1   *teaspoon hot red chili powder*
2   *tablespoons tamarind paste dissolved in $^1/_2$ cup water, strained (see How to Make, page 289)*
5   *fresh or dried curry leaves (available in Indian, Thai, or Southeast Asian markets)*
2   *small ripe tomatoes, cut into wedges (1 cup)*
3   *pounds fish heads, such as salmon, sea bass, or similar fish, halved and well rinsed*
5   *whole okra, tops and bottoms trimmed*

1.   Process the shallots, ginger, and garlic to a smooth paste with $^1/_4$ cup of the coconut milk.
2.   Heat the oil in a large pan, add the spice paste, cinnamon, star anise, cardamom, and cloves, and stir-fry over low heat 2 min-

utes. Add the curry powder, chili powder, and the balance of the coconut milk and combine well.

3. Bring the mixture to a boil and add the tamarind liquid, curry leaves, tomatoes, fish heads, and okra. Simmer the curry, covered, over low heat for 30 to 35 minutes, assuring yourself that the fish heads are cooked through. Baste the mixture several times during the cooking but do not stir. Transfer the curry to a large platter.

Serve warm with rice.

SERVES 8 WITH OTHER DISHES.

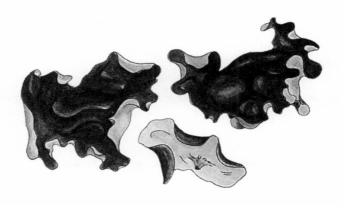

OTAK-OTAK (MALAY)

Steamed Fish Purée in Banana Leaves

These admirable appetizers are easy to assemble and are seasoned with traditional ingredients, the ubiquitous hot dried chili, coconut milk, lemongrass, and galangal. The recommended fish is fillet of mackerel or bluefish—dark fish with some natural oil.

The flat packages of banana leaves can be prepared well in advance, refrigerated, then steamed over hot water in a Chinese-style steamer. Delicious!

 1   *tablespoon hot red chili flakes, moistened with water*
 2   *stalks lemongrass, root end bulb only, sliced*
      a ¹/₂-inch piece galangal (see Glossary), sliced
 1   *medium onion, sliced (¹/₂ cup)*
 ¹/₂ *teaspoon turmeric*
 1¹/₂ *pounds fillet of mackerel or similar dark-fleshed fish, puréed*
 2   *kaffir lime leaves (available in Southeast Asian markets), sliced thin*
 2   *eggs, beaten*
 ³/₄ *cup "regular" coconut milk (see page 14)*
 8–10 *banana leaves, 6 × 14 inches in size (available fresh or frozen in some Asian markets, or see Note)*

1. Process the chili flakes, lemongrass, galangal, onion, and turmeric to a smooth paste. Combine well with the fish purée and add the lime leaves, eggs, and coconut milk. Combine well.

2. Divide the fish mixture into 8 or more portions of about ¹/₂ cup each. Place one portion in the center of each banana leaf and flatten it out into a slab 4 inches long, 2 inches wide and about ¹/₂ inch thick, or a bit less. (If the purée is too thick, then the filling may not be well enough cooked.)

3. Fold the banana leaves over *lengthwise*, smoothing out the package with your fingers. Push a toothpick about 2 inches from the

end through the leaf to seal the package, which should now remain flat from end to end.

Steam the packets, covered, over boiling water for 15 minutes. Or, as is frequently done, you can roast the packages over charcoal for 15 minutes, turning them over once.

Serve as an appetizer or as an additional dish in a Malaysian meal.

MAKES 8 TO 10 PACKAGES.

NOTE If you cannot locate banana leaves, use aluminum foil and follow the same directions above.

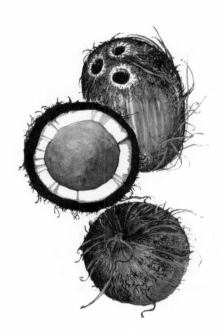

Ikan Tenggiri Gravy (Malay)

Fish and Spiced Sauce

This recipe is from Malacca and, as expected, has a touch of the colonial Portuguese to it, with its substantial array of spices and suggestion of sweet and sour opposition. The *tenggiri* is a local Malaysian fish that has been translated as "Spanish mackerel." My teacher in Malacca said that both red snapper and sea bass were legitimate substitutes.

1	*teaspoon ground coriander*
1	*teaspoon ground cumin*
1	*teaspoon ground fennel*
1	*tablespoon sliced ginger*
1	*tablespoon sliced galangal (see Glossary)*
½	*teaspoon turmeric*
2	*cups "regular" coconut milk (see page 14)*
2	*tablespoons corn oil*
1	*tablespoon tamarind paste dissolved in 3 tablespoons water, strained (see How to Make, page 289)*
2	*teaspoons brown sugar*
1	*tablespoon fresh lime juice*
½	*teaspoon salt, or to taste*
1	*tablespoon sliced and seeded fresh hot red chili*
1½	*pounds red snapper or sea bass, cut into 4 pieces*

1. Process the coriander, cumin, fennel, ginger, galangal, and turmeric with ½ cup of the coconut milk to a smooth paste.
2. Heat the oil in a wok or pan and stir-fry the spice paste over low heat until the aroma rises. Add the balance of the coconut milk, tamarind liquid, brown sugar, lime juice, salt, and fresh chili and bring the mixture to a boil.
3. Add the fish slices and simmer, covered, over low heat, basting now and then, for 15 minutes.

   Serve the fish and sauce warm with rice.

SERVES 4.

IKAN MASAK TEMPOYAK (MALAY)

Sea Bass in Fermented Durian

Here is a traditional Malay dish from the state of Perak. It is very unconventional, but has many aficionados.

The durian is a botanical native of Malaysia but is grown in several other tropical regions. It is notorious not only for its unpleasant aroma, but also for the esteem which people have for it. You either like it or don't. Cracking open the large prickly fruit, one finds a compelling creamy pulp. It is this pulp that is first fermented, then cooked with the sea bass.

³/₄ cup water
2 tablespoons tempoyak (fermented durian pulp, see Note)
3 stalks lemongrass, bottom 5 inches, cracked
¹/₂ teaspoon turmeric
¹/₄ teaspoon salt
2 fresh hot red chilis, seeded
1 tablespoon fresh milk (optional)
2 pounds sea bass, cut into 8 equal slices

Put all the ingredients, except the fish, in a pan. Bring to a boil, add the fish slices, and cover the pan. Simmer over low heat for 20 minutes, basting now and then.

Serve warm.

SERVES 8 WITH RICE.

NOTE How to Make *Tempoyak*

Remove the pulp from the prickly shell of several durian. Put the pulp in a bottle, cover the bottle, and allow the durian to ferment at room temperature for 3 days. Then whip the fermented fruit until it is the consistency of mayonnaise.

Ikan Panggang (all Malaysia)

Barbecued Fish

All the states of Malaysia have access to the sea and it follows that each has a continuous supply of fresh fish. And what easier way to prepare it than in the old traditional manner, with seasonings over charcoal. For modern homes, the fish may also be broiled in a gas oven or electric broiler, but charcoal is better.

The Fish

    a 2-pound whole fish, such as pomfret, flounder, or a similar fish, cleaned but with head on, and scored twice diagonally on both sides

1   *teaspoon salt*
1/4 *teaspoon pepper*
1   *teaspoon turmeric*
1   *tablespoon tamarind paste dissolved in 1/4 cup water, strained (see How to Make, page 289)*

The Sauce

2   *medium onions, sliced (1 cup)*
3   *cloves garlic, sliced*
1/4 *teaspoon* belacan, *toasted (see Glossary)*
1   *tablespoon* chili boh *(see How to Make, page 290)*
1   *tablespoon tamarind paste dissolved in 3 tablespoons water, strained (see above)*
1/2 *teaspoon sugar*
1/2 *teaspoon salt, or to taste*
1   *tablespoon vegetable oil*
2   *scallions, sliced thin*

1.   Prepare the fish: Mix all the ingredients, except the fish, together well. Rub the mixture into the fish and let it marinate for 1/2 hour.

2. Wrap the fish in a sheet of oiled aluminum foil. (The original traditional method was in a banana leaf.) Roast the whole fish over charcoal or in a gas or electric broiler for 15 minutes, turning it during the cooking time once.
3. Prepare the sauce: Process all the sauce ingredients, except the oil and scallions, to a smooth paste. Heat the oil in a wok or skillet and stir-fry the paste over low heat for 3 minutes, stirring continuously.
4. To serve, unwrap the fish on a platter, pour the sauce over the fish, and garnish with the scallions.

    Serve warm with rice and any kind of pickle.

SERVES 8.

IKAN KUKUS (CHINESE)

Steamed Whole Fish

A recipe of this sort—steamed fish, which is almost completely fat free—should be in every kitchen. It's a traditional Chinese preparation that is regional and has a number of flavorful ideas like oyster sauce, fresh hot chilis, and shallots. Very easy to assemble, the combination also fulfills our modern-day ideas about healthy eating.

	a 2-pound whole grouper, red snapper, sea bass, or similar fish, cleaned
1	*tablespoon light soy sauce*
1	*tablespoon white vinegar*
1	*tablespoon oyster sauce*
4–5	*fresh small red or green hot chilis, seeded and sliced, to taste*
2	*shallots, sliced*
1	*whole scallion*
1	*sprig fresh coriander*
1/4	*teaspoon salt*
1/8	*teaspoon pepper*
2	*tablespoons water*
1	*teaspoon vegetable oil*

1. Arrange the fish on a heatproof dish.
2. Mix all the remaining ingredients together and spread them over the fish.
3. Steam the fish, covered, over boiling water for 15 minutes. Moderate heat is recommended.

Serve hot with rice.

SERVES 6 TO 8.

VARIATION Two pounds large shrimp in the shell may be substituted for the whole fish above. Steam for 15 minutes and serve warm or at room temperature.

CHEONG CHING FEI CHOW (CHINESE)

Steamed Tilapia with Bean Sauce

The tilapia is a freshwater fish resembling a red snapper in appearance. When the tin industry in Malaysia began to fail, abandoned tin mines were filled with water. These freshwater manmade ponds or lakes became the source of introduced farm-raised fish.

Tilapia, also known as St. Peter's fish, are visible in tanks in restaurants where they are served. Since there is a large supply of freshwater in Malaysia, especially during the monsoon season, the sweet-fleshed fish is popular and available, from the tank to the table.

1   *tablespoon chopped ginger*
1   *scallion, chopped*
1   *tablespoon chopped onion*
2   *cloves garlic, chopped*
1   *teaspoon dried orange peel, soaked in water and shredded*
½   *teaspoon thinly sliced fresh hot red chili*
1   *teaspoon chopped canned pickled leek*
1   *tablespoon bottled bean sauce*
1   *teaspoon bottled plum sauce*
½   *teaspoon sugar*
     a 1½-pound whole tilapia or substitute red snapper or sea bass, cleaned and rinsed

1.   Mix all the ingredients, except the fish, together well.
2.   Put the fish on a porcelain or glass platter and pour the seasoning mix over it.
3.   Steam the fish, covered, over boiling water in a Chinese-style steamer for 15 to 20 minutes.

     Serve warm.

SERVES 4 TO 6.

FISH PASTE STUFFING FOR VEGETABLES AND TOFU (CHINESE)

This is an extremely useful recipe for the American homemaker. I noticed in the food courts in Ipoh and Penang that hawkers had at the ready stuffed tofu, green chili, and okra to serve as a garnish in noodle soup. Then there were the rough-skinned bitter melon and Asian eggplant that had been sliced, stuffed, and deep fried. A busy noodle soup shop lady told me that she preferred to steam the stuffed vegetables over hot water, which should take about 15 minutes.

½ *pound fish fillet, such as flounder or red snapper, sliced*
½ *teaspoon salt*
¼ *teaspoon sugar*
2 *egg whites*
1½ *tablespoons cornstarch*
1 *teaspoon cold water*
1 *tablespoon chopped scallion*
2 *okra*
2 *each green and red fresh hot chilis*
2 *soft or Japanese-style tofu, cut into 2 rectangles each*

1. Process the fish, salt, sugar, egg whites, cornstarch, and water to a smooth purée. Add the scallion and stir it into the paste.
2. Cut a 2-inch slit in each okra. Fill the slits with about 2 teaspoons of the fish paste and smooth over the incision. Fill the chilis in the same manner but scoop out as many seeds as possible before stuffing them to reduce the heat.
3. Cut a slit in the tofu rectangles. Open the slits carefully and stuff with 1 generous tablespoon of the fish paste.

4. The stuffed items may be boiled in soup, deep fried in hot oil, or steamed for about 15 minutes. They can be served in soup with or without noodles. As a more modern touch, the cooked stuffed vegetables and tofu may be served as an appetizer with drinks and a favorite dip.

MAKES ABOUT ½ CUP FISH PASTE STUFFING.

Nasi Kandar (Indian Muslim)

Fish Curry and Rice

In the good old days, street hawkers carried their curries and rice in two baskets, neatly balanced over their shoulder. The stout pole that supported all this was made from *kandar*, a local wood, and the dish was given that name, the same name it is still known by today.

The Rice

2   *pounds long-grain rice, well rinsed in cold water*

The Curry

 3   *tablespoons corn oil*
 2   *medium onions, chopped (1 cup)*
 5   *fresh or dried curry leaves (available in Indian, Thai, or Southeast Asian markets)*
 2   *pounds grouper, sea bass, or red snapper, cut into 8 slices*
 1/4 *cup tamarind paste dissolved in 2/3 cup water, strained (see How to Make, page 289)*
 2   *tablespoons curry powder*
 1/2 *teaspoon turmeric*
 1/2 *teaspoon chili powder*
 1/2 *teaspoon salt*
 3   *cups water*
 2   *ripe tomatoes (1/2 pound), cut into 4 wedges each*
 2   *fresh hot green chilis, seeded and halved lengthwise*
 2   *fresh hot red chilis, seeded and halved lengthwise*
16   *okra, 2 per person, ends trimmed*

1.   Prepare the rice: Cook the rice in the conventional manner or in a rice cooker. Set aside.
2.   Prepare the curry: Heat the oil in a pan, add the onions and

curry leaves, and stir-fry over low heat until the onions turn golden.

3. Put the fish in a separate pan with the tamarind liquid, curry powder, turmeric, chili powder, salt, and water. Mix well and add it to the pan with the onions. Bring the liquid to a boil, cover the pan, and simmer over low heat for 10 minutes.

4. Uncover the pan, add the tomatoes, green and red chilis, and okra, and simmer for 3 minutes. Cover the pan again, remove it from the heat, and set it aside for 20 minutes. Then reheat, bringing it to a boil before serving.

Serve warm with white rice and a side dish of fruit and vegetables (see below).

SERVES 8.

VARIATION The same curry can be made with 2 pounds boneless lamb, beef, or chicken parts. The timing will be longer for a meat curry.

SIDE DISH

1 *cup cubed ripe pineapple (1/2-inch pieces)*
2 *small onions, peeled and sliced in rings*
2 *young cucumbers, not peeled, cut into cubes*
2 *fresh hot red chilis, seeded and sliced thin*

Mix all the ingredients together without seasoning. Serve as a side dish with the curry and rice.

Ikan Asam Pedas
(Indian Muslim, Kuching)

Sour and Hot Fish

Fresh fish in Sarawak is always available and any preparation there has this advantage over faraway countries that rely on frozen foods and the other fast-food abominations of the twentieth century.

The Fish

3   *tablespoons vegetable oil*
1   *stalk lemongrass, bottom 4 inches, cracked*
    a 1-inch piece ginger, sliced
2   *cloves garlic, sliced*
2   *whole dried hot red chilis*
1   *large onion, sliced (1 cup)*
2   *shallots, sliced*
2   *pounds red snapper, pomfret, or similar fish, cut into 5 slices*

The Sauce

1   *tablespoon white vinegar*
1   *tablespoon soy sauce*
1   *teaspoon sugar*
1   *tablespoon tomato paste*
1   *tablespoon tomato ketchup*
1/2   *cup water*

1. Prepare the fish: Heat the oil in a skillet, and add all the ingredients, except the fish. Stir-fry over low heat for 3 minutes.
2. Place the fish slices in the skillet and fry for 2 minutes on each side. Set aside off the heat for a moment.

3. Prepare the sauce: Mix all the sauce ingredients together.
4. Pour the sauce over the fish in the skillet and simmer over low heat, covered, for 5 minutes, basting the fish several times.
   Serve warm with rice.

SERVES 4 TO 6.

SWEET AND SOUR FISH (NONYA OF MALACCA)

The Nonya go their own culinary way, absorbing little bits of crosscultural influences from Europe, China, and the Malay states.

¼ cup cornstarch
½ teaspoon salt
1 egg, beaten
1 pound boneless grouper, red snapper, or similar fish, cut into 4 slices
1 cup vegetable oil for deep frying
1 tablespoon sugar
¼ teaspoon hot red chili powder
3 tablespoons tomato sauce
2 tablespoons white vinegar
1 tablespoon bottled plum sauce
¾ cup water
1 young cucumber, not peeled, cut into ¼-inch cubes, for garnish

1. Mix the cornstarch, salt, and egg together. Add the fish slices and toss to coat well.
2. Heat enough oil for deep frying in a wok and fry the fish slices, one by one, over low heat until light brown. Remove and keep warm.
3. Mix the sugar, chili powder, tomato sauce, vinegar, and plum sauce in a bowl.
4. Add the water to the wok, bring to a boil over low heat, and add the sugar/vinegar mixture. Simmer slowly for 5 minutes as the sauce thickens.

   To serve, put the warm fish slices on a serving platter and pour the sauce over them. Garnish with the cucumber cubes.

SERVES 4.

VARIATION This recipe can be prepared with one whole fish weighing about
1¹/₂ pounds. Use the same amount of seasonings. A whole fish does
have a more impressive appearance than the slices but the flavor is the
same.

Dip the whole fish in the cornstarch/egg mixture and deep fry it for
5 minutes until brown and crisp. Place the fish on a serving platter,
pour the sauce over it, and garnish with the cucumber cubes.

SERVES 4.

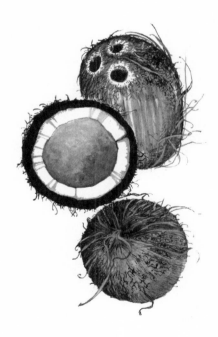

BAKED FISH MALACCA STYLE (PORTUGUESE)

The Portuguese conquered Malacca in 1511 on one of their colonial sprees, and the result in 1997 is a identifiably regional cuisine in Malacca that has developed over the centuries and can be noted as such. A number of dishes can be very chili-hot, so one must be prepared for the variable intensity of chili wherever one happens to live. In this recipe I have taken the liberty of reducing the number of chilis by half, and it still retains a wallop.

5   *fresh hot red chilis, seeded and sliced*
5   *shallots, sliced*
8   kemiri *(macadamia nuts)*
1   *cup "regular" coconut milk (see page 14)*
2   *tablespoons vegetable oil*
2   *tablespoons fresh lime juice*
2   *kaffir lime leaves (available in Southeast Asian markets), sliced into*
      julienne strips
½   *teaspoon salt*
½   *teaspoon sugar*
      a 2-pound whole sea bass, tilapia, or red snapper, cleaned, or a 2-pound
      chunk sting ray
1   *rectangular banana leaf*
1   *piece aluminum foil, 14 × 16 inches*

1.   Process the chilis, shallots, and *kemiri* with ¼ cup of the coconut milk to a smooth paste.
2.   Heat the oil in a pan and stir-fry the paste over low heat for 2 minutes which releases its aroma. Add the balance of the coconut milk, lime juice, lime leaves, salt, and sugar and simmer over low heat for 5 minutes.

3. Dip the fish in the sauce, then remove it to the banana leaf centered on the piece of aluminum foil. Pour the balance of the sauce over the fish and fold the foil over carefully to completely seal in the contents.
4. Bake the fish in a preheated 325-degree oven for ½ hour.
    Unwrap the package and serve warm with rice.

SERVES 6 OR MORE WITH OTHER DISHES.

CHOP CHAI #1
(MALACCA PORTUGUESE/NONYA)

Chop Suey

A literal translation of a dish that has crosscultural beginnings, this one is simple to assemble and useful to know as a side dish with other Malaysian foods. It is often served with Sambal Belacan side dish (page 245).

The necessary ingredients—fish balls, fish cake, brown bean paste, dried tofu sticks, and cellophane noodles—can all be purchased ready to use in Chinese groceries.

2   tablespoons vegetable oil
3   cloves garlic, chopped fine
1   tablespoon bottled ground brown bean paste
¼   cup water
4   strips of thick, dried tofu sticks (also known as dried bean thread) soaked in water ½ hour, drained, and cut into 1-inch pieces
1   bundle (about 3 ounces) cellophane noodles, soaked in water ½ hour and drained
½   pound green or red cabbage, cut into 2-inch pieces
6   fish balls (page 192), halved
6   slices ground fish loaf (available in Chinese markets, in the fresh or frozen sections)
10 pieces cloud ears (black fungus) soaked in water 1 hour, changing water twice, drained, and sliced into julienne strips
2   tablespoons black soy sauce (kicip in Malay, see Glossary)
½   teaspoon sugar

1.   Heat the oil in a wok or large pan, add the garlic, and stir-fry a moment over low heat to brown. Stir in the bean paste and water and combine.

2. Add all the remaining ingredients and stir-fry over low heat for 5 minutes, enough time to integrate the flavors and heat through the ingredients.

     Serve warm with rice.

SERVES 8.

UMAI (ETHNIC PEOPLE, SARAWAK)

Fish in Lime Juice

Latin America is another region where fresh fish is "cooked" in fresh lime juice. This recipe is a local dish prepared by the Dayak Iban, but obviously developed independently from that, in Peru or Mexico.

1   *pound fresh skinless fillet of red snapper, sea bass, or similar fish*
¼   *cup fresh lime juice*
4   *cloves garlic, sliced thin*
4   *shallots, sliced thin*
2   *fresh hot red chilis, seeded and sliced into julienne strips*
    a 2-inch piece young ginger, sliced into julienne strips
½   *teaspoon* belacan, *toasted (see Glossary), dissolved in 1 teaspoon water*
½   *teaspoon salt, or to taste*
⅛   *teaspoon pepper*

1. Cut each fillet crosswise into thin 2-inch-long slices. Add the lime juice and stir it into the fish slices in a bowl. Then add the garlic, shallots, chilis, ginger, and *belacan* and mix well. Add the salt and pepper.

2. Cover and refrigerate until ready to serve, after 15 minutes and up to 30 minutes. Longer is better.

    Serve as a first course with any meal or as a snack.

SERVES 5 OR 6.

HINAVA (ETHNIC PEOPLE, SABAH)

Kadazan Ceviche

The Kadazan are an indigenous people of Sabah, one of the two Malaysian states on the island of Borneo (the other is Sarawak). They are a people close to nature, but have moved into the twentieth century with aplomb and success. I visited a *kampong* (village) not too far from Kota Kinabalu, the capital of Sabah, and was treated to a variety of ethnic dishes.

The Kadazan are essentially fish-eaters although *por*, beef and chicken, are the principal meats. Contrary to uninformed wags, this is not the region to sample crocodile curry or other exotic dishes.

Surprisingly, as a lesson in geographical distances, the Kadazan prepare ceviche just as they do in Central and South America, "cooking" the fish in a generous amount of fresh lime juice.

2   *pounds fresh mackerel, flounder, red snapper, or similar skinless fillets*
    a 2-inch piece ginger, sliced thin
5   *shallots, sliced thin*
1   *clove garlic, sliced thin*
2   *fresh hot red chilis, seeded and sliced thin*
½   *cup lime juice (about 5 limes)*
½   *teaspoon salt*

1. Slice the raw fish very thin, into 2-inch-long pieces. Add the ginger, shallots, garlic, chilis, and the lime juice to the fish in the bowl, and toss well to integrate the juice and cook the fish.
2. Cover and let stand for at least 15 minutes but ½ hour or longer is better. Refrigerate.

    Best served as a snack or salad side dish.

SERVES 6.

UDANG GALAH SAMBAL (MALAY/INDIAN)

Freshwater Prawns in Tamarind Hot Sauce

Galah are the large freshwater prawns that are found in the farms in Pahang state on the east coast of Malaysia. There are three or four to the pound and much desired. Sometimes they can be seen cooked in display windows of Malay restaurants.

For this recipe I have called for jumbo tiger prawns from the sea. Their flavor is stronger than the freshwater variety but they are always available in fish stores.

5   *shallots, sliced*
    a ¹/₂-inch piece ginger, sliced
3   *cloves garlic, sliced*
¹/₄ teaspoon belacan, *toasted (see Glossary)*
¹/₄ *cup water*
2   *tablespoons vegetable oil*
1   *tablespoon hot chili paste (see Note)*
¹/₄ *cup tamarind paste dissolved in ¹/₂ cup water, strained (see How to Make, page 289)*
¹/₂ *teaspoon sugar*
¹/₄ *teaspoon salt*
2   *pounds jumbo tiger prawns in their shell*

1. Process the shallots, ginger, garlic, and *belacan* with the water to a smooth paste.
2. Heat the oil in a wok or large skillet and add the hot chili paste and shallot paste. Stir-fry over low heat for 2 minutes. Add the tamarind liquid, sugar, salt, and prawns and stir-fry another 3 to 4 minutes, just until the prawns are cooked through.

    Serve warm with rice and side dishes.

    SERVES 6 TO 8.

VARIATION Crab may be substituted for the tiger prawns. The Malaysian flower crab is tender with a soft shell that can be easily broken. The Maryland crab has a much firmer shell and is not as sweet, but it makes a good replacement with the seasonings.

NOTE To make hot chili paste: In a saucepan, combine $1/4$ pound hot red dried chilis, broken up, seeds removed, with $1/2$ cup water and simmer them together over low heat until the chilis are soft and malleable, about 10 minutes. Then process the mixture in a blender to a paste. The paste can be refrigerated in a jar with a tight cover for several weeks. It is this paste that is used in the sambal.

PINAASAKAN (ETHNIC PEOPLE, SABAH)

Fish Stew

Formerly, this dish was prepared by the Kadazan people in Sabah with freshwater river fish, but since saltwater fish are easily available, the stew is now made with both fresh and saltwater fish.

1   *whole 2-pound fish, any kind*
1   *fresh turmeric leaf (optional)*
2   *tablespoons tamarind paste dissolved in ¹/₂ cup water, strained (see How to Make, page 289)*
3   *cloves garlic, sliced*
      a 1-inch piece ginger, sliced
¹/₂   *teaspoon salt, or to taste*
2   *ripe tomatoes, cut into wedges (1 cup)*
³/₄   *cup water*

Score the fish twice diagonally on each side. Put it in the bottom of a pan and arrange the remaining ingredients over it. Bring the liquid to a boil over low heat, cover the pan, and simmer for 15 to 20 minutes.

Or, you can also cook the fish longer, until almost all the liquid has evaporated, for a drier stew.

Serve warm with rice.

SERVES 6 OR MORE.

SOTONG MASAK KICUP (MALAY)

Squid in Black Sauce

Do not be intimidated by the seventeen necessary ingredients, or the spices and seasonings that are required in this recipe. Nuances are often what matters in this Ipoh-style cooking, which combines Chinese and Malay techniques illustrating the multicultural culinary ideas in Malaysia.

1/4 cup corn oil
4 shallots, sliced
4 cloves garlic, sliced
   a 1/2-inch piece ginger, sliced
2 stalks lemongrass, bottom 5 inches, cracked
2 cardamom pods
   a 1-inch piece cinnamon stick
2 teaspoons hot red chili powder
2 teaspoons curry powder
2 tablespoons oyster sauce
2 tablespoons black soy sauce (kicip in Malay, see Glossary)
2 pounds whole small squid, cleaned and rinsed well
1/2 cup chopped ripe tomato
1 fresh hot red chili, sliced thin
1 fresh hot green chili, sliced thin
1/2 teaspoon salt
1/2 teaspoon sugar

1. Heat the oil in a wok or pan, add the shallots, garlic, and ginger, and stir-fry until light brown over moderate heat. Add the lemongrass, cardamom, cinnamon stick, chili powder, and curry powder and continue to stir-fry until combined.

2. Add the oyster and black soy sauces, then add the small squid and mix well. Lastly, stir in the tomato, red and green chilis, salt and sugar and stir-fry for 5 minutes.

   Serve warm with rice.

SERVES 8.

SHRIMP WITH CHILI AND GINGER (CHINESE)

This is a local recipe from Kuala Lumpur, the capital of Malaysia. It is homecooking for no special event, just when the mood dictates.

2   *tablespoons vegetable oil*
1   *pound fresh shrimp, peeled and deveined*
    a ¹/₂-inch piece ginger, chopped
1   *clove garlic, smashed with the flat side of a cleaver*
1–2 teaspoons chili boh *(see How to Make, page 290), to taste*
1   *scallion, sliced thin*
2   *tablespoons bottled chili sauce*
¹/₃ *cup chopped ripe tomato, or 2 tablespoons tomato sauce*
1   *teaspoon black soy sauce (*kicip *in Malay, see Glossary)*
¹/₂ *teaspoon sugar*
¹/₄ *cup chicken broth combined with ¹/₂ teaspoon cornstarch*

1. Heat the oil in a wok or skillet, add the shrimp, and stir-fry over moderate heat for 1 minute. Remove the shrimp and set aside.
2. To the same oil, add the ginger, garlic, *chili boh*, and scallion and stir-fry for 1 minute. Add the chili sauce, tomato, soy sauce, and sugar and continue to stir-fry until combined.
3. Add the shrimp and chicken broth mixture and simmer over low heat for 2 to 3 minutes to thicken the sauce.
    Serve warm with rice.

SERVES 4 TO 6 WITH OTHER DISHES.

ASAM UDANG (CHINESE)

Tamarind Shrimp

Tamarind is that universally appreciated fruit seasoning that can be found in tropical Asia and Central and South America. Its acidic flavor cannot be duplicated, although one can make an imperfect substitute. This Penang dish is Chinese in origin.

3   *pounds medium shrimp, peeled and deveined*
¼   *cup tamarind paste dissolved in ½ cup water, strained (see How to Make, page 289)*
1   *tablespoon sugar*
3   *pounds medium shrimp, peeled and deveined*
1   *tablespoon sugar*
1   *teaspoon salt*
1   *teaspoon pepper*
⅓   *cup corn oil*

1. Marinate the shrimp in ¼ cup of the tamarind liquid with the salt, the sugar, and pepper for ½ hour. Drain and discard the marinade.

2. Heat the oil in a wok or large skillet, add the shrimp, and stir-fry over high heat for 2 minutes. Add the balance of the tamarind liquid and stir-fry for 2 minutes. This is a dry stir-fry; there is no sauce.

   Serve warm.

SERVES 8 WITH STEAMED RICE AND PICKLED GINGER (PAGE 240) OR CUCUMBER PICKLE (PAGE 241).

SOTONG CHILI (CHINESE)

Squid with Chili

Each region has its own seasonings and flavorings. A dish is called "local" when it is special to a particular locality. This is a local squid recipe cooked by the Chinese their way in Kota Bahru, the capital of Kelantan state. That's it!

  2 *cups water*
  2 *pounds medium squid, the bodies cut into ¹/₂-inch-wide round slices*
  2 *tablespoons corn oil*
5–6 *hot red dried chilis, to taste*
  1 *tablespoon black soy sauce* (kicip *in Malay, see Glossary*)
  2 *tablespoons white vinegar*
 ¹/₂ *teaspoon salt*
 ¹/₂ *teaspoon sugar*
  2 *teaspoons bottled chili sauce (see Note)*
  1 *tablespoon sesame oil*

1. Bring the water to a rapid boil in a large pan, add the squid, and cook over high heat for 2 minutes. Drain.
2. Heat the oil in a wok or large skillet and stir-fry the whole chilis over low heat for ¹/₂ minute. Add the blanched squid, soy sauce, vinegar, salt, sugar, and chili sauce and stir-fry over low heat for 3 minutes. Stir in the sesame oil.

    Serve warm with rice.

SERVES 8.

NOTE There are several bottled chili sauces available in Malaysia as well as in New York's Chinatown. They are piquant and red in color, with seasonings, but no tomato. The color is from red chilis. To my knowledge, in Malaysia chili sauce is not prepared at home when it can be so easily purchased.

Prawn Varuval (Indian)

Dry Prawn Roast

Prawns are shrimp, but "prawn" is the word that is used in Malaysia. This dry fry is traditionally served as a main dish with rice; however, it works very well as an appetizer with drinks.

¼ cup corn oil
1 tablespoon chopped young ginger
1 tablespoon chopped garlic
2 medium onions, thinly sliced (1 cup plus)
2 pounds medium prawns, peeled and deveined
3–4 tablespoons hot red chili powder, to taste
1 teaspoon turmeric
¼ teaspoon salt
1 tablespoon light soy sauce
½ teaspoon black soy sauce (kicip in Malay, see Glossary)

1. Heat the oil in a large skillet, add the ginger and garlic, and stir-fry a minute over low heat. Add the onions and stir-fry until the onions start to brown.

2. Add the prawns and stir-fry, tossing well, for 5 minutes. Add the chili powder, turmeric, salt, and light and dark soy sauces and mix well. There is no sauce. The seasonings will coat the prawns.

    Serve warm or at room temperature.

SERVES 8 WITH OTHER DISHES.

Udang Lamat Nanas
(Nonya and Portuguese)

Shrimp and Pineapple in Coconut Milk Sauce

The Nonya and colonial Portuguese run a parallel course in Malacca, so it is logical that there is a crosscultural coincidence in establishing a particular recipe. This combination of shrimp and pineapple is inspired, and so easily accessible to the American kitchen that its acceptance is a foregone conclusion.

3–4   *hot red dried chilis, to taste, seeded*
5   kemiri *(macadamia nuts)*
¼   *teaspoon turmeric*
¼   *teaspoon* belacan, *toasted (see Glossary)*
    a ¹/₂-inch piece galangal (see Glossary), sliced
1   *medium onion, sliced (¹/₂ cup)*
¼   *teaspoon salt*
1   *cup "regular" coconut milk (see page 14)*
2   *tablespoons corn oil*
¼   *cup water*
2   *stalks lemongrass, bottom 5 inches, cracked (see Note)*
1½   *cups cubed fresh ripe pineapple (1-inch pieces)*
1   *pound medium shrimp, peeled and deveined*

1. Process the chilis, macadamia nuts, turmeric, *belacan,* galangal, onion, and salt moistened with 3 tablespoons of the coconut milk to a relatively smooth paste.

2. Heat the oil in a wok or pan and stir-fry the spice paste over low heat until the aroma rises, about 3 minutes. Add the balance of the coconut milk, water, lemongrass, and pineapple and bring to a boil, combining well. Add the shrimp and simmer over low heat for 3 minutes. Adjust the sugar and salt if necessary.

    Serve warm.

SERVES 6 OR MORE WITH RICE.

NOTE When lemongrass is fresh, as it is in Malaysia where often the cook
      can step into the yard and harvest a stalk, the lower 3 or 4 inches are
      soft and malleable. In this case, the grass is then sliced thin and in-
      cluded in the spice paste where it can be reduced smoothly. However,
      in most cases in New York City, the lemongrass available is too firm
      to do this. It then should be cracked with a firm blow or two and
      added to the sauce, where its flavor will disperse.

Udang Goreng Sambal (Ethnic People, Sabah)

Deep-Fried Shrimp with Chili Sauce

This is a "local" recipe of the people of Kota Kinabalu, Sabah, that is to say, it is a known dish in the city and many people cook it in this manner.

The Shrimp

2	*pounds medium shrimp, with heads and tails on*
1	*teaspoon salt*
1	*teaspoon turmeric*
1/8	*teaspoon pepper*
1	*tablespoon tamarind paste dissolved in 3 tablespoons water, strained (see How to Make, page 289)*
1	*cup vegetable oil for deep frying*

The Sauce

3	*medium onions, sliced (1 1/2 cups)*
3	*cloves garlic, sliced*
1/4	*teaspoon* belacan, *toasted (see Glossary)*
2	*tablespoons* chili boh *(see How to Make, page 290)*
1	*tablespoon tamarind paste dissolved in 3 tablespoons water, strained (see above)*
1	*teaspoon sugar*
1/2	*teaspoon salt*
1/8	*teaspoon pepper*
1	*tablespoon corn oil*
2	*scallions, sliced thin, for garnish*

1. Prepare the shrimp: Marinate the shrimp in the salt, turmeric, pepper, and tamarind juice for 1/2 hour. Mix well.
2. Heat the oil in a wok or skillet and stir-fry the shrimp over moderate heat for 1 minute. Remove with a slotted spoon and set aside.
3. Prepare the sauce: Process all the sauce ingredients, except the oil and scallions, to a smooth paste.
4. Heat the oil in a wok or skillet and stir-fry the spice paste over low heat for 3 minutes. Add the shrimp, toss well, and stir-fry for 3 minutes. Garnish with the scallions.

   Serve warm.

SERVES 8 WITH RICE AND OTHER DISHES.

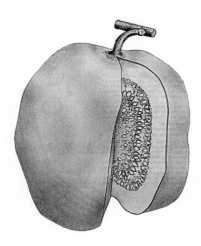

VEGETARIAN DISHES

Malaysians are not really vegetarians as though vegetarianism were a cult one joined. Some are, of course, due to religious persuasion (Hindu Indians); others are genuinely committed to removing meat

Giant okra in Sabah market.

and seafood from their diets. Then there are the various stages of vegetarianism, which is to say that the diet one selects is due to personal preference, and there are many nonmeat dishes in this cuisine to fill the gap. (Note: Recipes in this section which contain animal products are noted.)

In addition, a tropical country can provide and does produce any kind of commercial vegetable along with a host of edible greens from backyards or the surrounding countryside. My own experience with *pakis* (Wild Jungle Fern Stir Fry with Belacan, page 173) was a happy discovery that became a constant source of good taste. That there are edible greens growing everywhere and known to the indigenous population is a culinary advantage not to be overlooked.

Sayur Masak Lemak (Malay)

Savory Vegetable Sauté

Malaysian (also Burmese) vegetarian dishes often include dried shrimp to give them more dimension of taste. You can include four or all five of the vegetables below or double up on one or two that you particularly favor. (This recipe contains dried shrimp.)

2   cups "regular" coconut milk (see page 14)
5   shallots, sliced
3   cloves garlic, sliced
2   stalks lemongrass, bottom 5 inches, cracked
½   teaspoon salt
¼   teaspoon pepper
¼   teaspoon turmeric
1   tablespoon dried shrimp (available in Chinese groceries)
1   cup 1-inch wedges Oriental eggplant
1   cup sliced carrot (cut diagonally) ¼ inch thick
1   cup 1-inch pieces longbeans
1   cup coarsely shredded green cabbage
1   cup cubed peeled pumpkin or butternut squash (in ½-inch pieces)
     a 2-ounce package cellophane noodles, softened in water and drained
     (optional)

1. Put the coconut milk in a pan with the shallots, garlic, lemongrass, salt, pepper, turmeric, and shrimp and bring to a boil over low heat. Simmer for 5 minutes.
2. Add the 4 or 5 cups chopped vegetables and continue to simmer, covered, for 10 minutes for a crunchy texture, or 15 minutes for a softer one. Adjust the salt if necessary. Stir in the cellophane noodles, if using.

    Serve warm with rice.

SERVES 8.

Ulam Ulam (Malay)

Assorted Vegetables and Greens

Ulam ulam is a side dish frequently found on platters to accompany the main meal. This one is from Kota Bahru. When the assortment of hot curries and liberally spiced dishes is served, a platter of vegetables (always referred to as veggies), with or without a sauce, is a refreshing contrast. Recommended for those who enjoy it is the dip Sambal Belacan (page 236), which is traditional.

okra, briefly steamed or blanched in hot water and cut into 2-inch pieces
longbeans (loobia), *cut into 2-inch pieces, briefly steamed or raw*
Chinese greens, such as bok choy
lettuce leaves
cucumber slices
ulam raja *(wild ferns or fiddlehead ferns) in season*
cabbage pieces, blanched or raw

Serve at room temperature.

SAYUR CAMPUR (CHINESE)
Mixed Vegetable Stir-Fry

With its salubrious tropical climate, everything grows well in Malaysia. Fresh baby corn, called for here, is found in generous quantities in the public markets. Anything needed to fulfill the traditional characteristics of a recipe are immediately available, which makes planning a meal easy.

4   *cups water*
1   *cup cauliflower florets*
1   *cup sliced carrot (cut diagonally ¼ inch thick)*
6   *baby corn, halved lengthwise*
6   *dried black mushrooms, soaked in water 1 hour, drained, and halved*
12 *snow peas*
1   *tablespoon vegetable oil*
3   *cloves garlic, chopped*
¼   *cup vegetable or chicken broth*
4   *tablespoons oyster sauce*
⅛   *teaspoon pepper*
1   *teaspoon cornstarch dissolved in 2 tablespoons water*
1   *teaspoon sesame oil*

1. Bring the water to a rapid boil in a large saucepan. Blanch the cauliflower, carrot, corn, and black mushrooms for 1 minute. Add the snow peas and blanch for ½ minute. Drain.

2. Heat the oil in a wok and stir-fry the garlic over moderate heat until brown. Add the chicken broth, oyster sauce, pepper, and then the cornstarch mixture. Continue to stir-fry until the sauce thickens slightly.

3. Now add all the blanched vegetables and stir-fry for 2 minutes. Pour the sesame oil over all.
    Serve warm with rice.

    SERVES 4.

TAHU SUMBAT (CHINESE)

Stuffed Bean Curd

Tahu (tofu, bean curd) — that great protein invention that is ubiquitous in Asia — has many faces. The Malaysian way of cooking it is to brown the squares in oil, cut them in half diagonally, cut a slit in the soft part of each half, and stuff it with chopped vegetables. Then glorify the triangles with a rich, spicy uncooked peanut sauce, vivid with seasoning, and eat them as a snack at room temperature. That is *tahu sumbat* in a nutshell or, perhaps, a peanut shell.

The Tahu

1   *cup oil for deep frying*
6   *Chinese (firm) bean curd squares*
1/2 *cup bean sprouts, blanched briefly in boiling water and drained*
1/2 *cup shredded young cucumber, unpeeled*
1/2 *cup shredded jícama (see Glossary)*
1/4 *cup shredded lettuce*

The Peanut Sauce

1   *whole fresh or dried hot red chili, seeded*
1   *clove garlic, sliced*
1   *shallot, sliced*
1   *teaspoon vegetable oil*
1/2 *cup roasted peanuts, coarsely chopped*
1/4 *teaspoon* belacan, *toasted (see Glossary)*
1   *teaspoon tamarind paste dissolved in 2 tablespoons water, strained (see How to Make, page 289)*
2–3 *tablespoons sugar, to taste, or 1 tablespoon* gula Malacca *(see Glossary)*

1.   Prepare the *tahu:* Heat the oil in a wok or deep-frying pan and brown each bean curd square on both sides. Remove from the

oil to drain on paper towels, cool, and cut in half diagonally into 2 triangles. Cut a 2-inch slit in the soft center of each cut half. Set aside.

2. Mix the bean sprouts, cucumber, jícama, and lettuce together into a stuffing. Open the slits with your fingers and stuff about 2 tablespoons stuffing firmly into each bean half. Transfer to a serving platter.

3. Prepare the sauce: If you use the fresh chili, simply crush it in a mortar and pestle. If you use the dried chili, soak it in warm water to soften, then drain. Crush the chili, garlic, and shallot together.

2. In a small skillet heat the oil until hot and stir-fry the garlic-shallot paste until fragrant, about a minute.

4. Combine the paste with all the remaining ingredients into a thick sauce. Should the sauce be too chili-hot, then add more sugar to lessen the intensity. You can also add a tablespoon of hot water.

   Serve the sauce in a separate bowl. (Diners help themselves to *tahu* and sauce.)

SERVES 6.

CHOP CHAI #2 (HAKKA CHINESE)

Dried and Fresh Mixed Vegetables

Everything about this complete vegetarian homecooking spells health and good taste. Dried fungi, mushrooms, and dried day lily flowers when reconstituted in water are filled with flavor. Even the cellophane noodles are made from high-protein mung beans. And the fresh vegetables provide texture in contrast to everything else. In contrast, see page 137 for Chop Chai #1.

2	*black fungi (also known as wood ears, see Glossary)*
1/2	*cup dried day lily flowers (also known as golden needles)*
3	*dried black Chinese mushrooms, rinsed well*
2	*dried tofu skin sticks (see Glossary)*
2	*tablespoons vegetable oil*
	a 1 1/2-inch piece ginger, coarsely chopped into 1/4-inch pieces
3	*shallots, sliced*
2	*cloves garlic, sliced*
2	*tablespoons black soy sauce* (kicip *in Malay, see Glossary*)
1	*teaspoon salt, or to taste*
1/2	*teaspoon sugar*
1/4	*teaspoon pepper*
1	*teaspoon bottled ground brown bean paste*
1	*package (1 1/2 ounces) cellophane noodles, soaked in water 1/2 hour, drained*
1	*medium carrot, cut into julienne strips (1/2 cup)*
1 1/2	*cups shredded red or green cabbage, tender center leaves only*
2	*scallions, cut into 2-inch pieces*

1. Soak the fungi in water to cover for 2 hours. Drain and rinse well, changing the water two times to eliminate all of the sand. Then slice into julienne strips. Soak the day lily flowers in water to cover for 1 hour, drain, and trim off the hard stem ends. Soak the black mushrooms in 2 cups hot water 1 hour. *Reserve*

the soaking liquid, straining it through a metal sieve to remove any sand. Break the dried tofu skins in half and soak in a large amount of water for 1 hour, or more, to soften. Drain and cut in 2-inch pieces. Set aside.

2. Heat the oil in a wok, add the ginger, and stir-fry it over low heat until brown and crisp, about 2 minutes. Remove and set aside.

3. Add the shallots and garlic to the same oil and stir-fry until light brown. Add the Chinese black mushrooms and stir-fry 1 minute. Add the black fungi, lily flowers, and broken tofu sticks and stir-fry until combined. Add the soy sauce, salt, sugar, and pepper.

4. Now add the reserved mushroom soaking liquid, not more than 1 cup, and brown bean paste and bring to a boil. Stir-fry over low heat for 5 minutes. Add the noodles and mix well, tossing, for 2 minutes.

5. Add the carrot, cabbage, scallions, and reserved crisp ginger and toss well.

    Serve warm.

SERVES 6.

NOTE All dried items—the fungi, day lily flowers, mushrooms, and tofu skin sticks—along with the ground bean paste are available in Chinese food stores.

BINDE (INDIAN)

Split Pea Curry with Okra

Malacca is charming, well-behaved, and antique, with a knowledge of its colonial past, the Portuguese, Dutch, and British. With a little judicious investigation, I was able to discover its banana-leaf restaurants, with their authentic south Indian–Malaysian dishes, both vegetarian and with meat. Freshly prepared *thosai*, the fermented rice pancakes, are served to order with *dal*, the spiced split pea (or lentil) gruel, and heaps of rice, or anything else that is visibly displayed in steam-table containers. By one o'clock lunch was over, practically nothing was available, and the manager/owners sat at a table visiting with cronies, chattering away in their incomprehensible (to me) Tamil with Malacca conviviality.

What caught my eye and palate were the lady fingers, sometimes called okra, *bamiya*, and *binde*, in a stunning curry. Here it is.

1   *cup yellow split peas, well rinsed*
4   *cups water*
2   *pounds fresh okra (lady fingers), trimmed and cut into ¹/₂-inch pieces*
3   *tablespoons corn oil*
1   *teaspoon black mustard seed*
1–2 *tablespoons hot red chili powder, to taste*
3   *tablespoons ground coriander*
1   *teaspoon salt, or to taste*
2   *medium onions, sliced thin (1 cup)*
4   *cloves garlic, chopped*

1. Soak the split peas in the water for 2 hours. Bring to a boil and simmer over low heat until the peas are soft. Process the mixture into a smooth purée and set aside.
2. Put the okra in a Teflon wok or pan and stir-fry without oil over low heat for about 3 minutes. Remove and set aside. (This precooking is designed to prevent the okra from becoming gummy.)

3. Heat the oil in a pan over moderate heat and drop the mustard seed in. When they pop, immediately add the chili powder, coriander, salt, onions, and garlic and stir-fry for 2 minutes as the onion changes color.
4. Add the split pea purée and stir together well. Add the okra and simmer over low heat for 5 minutes, enough to soften them and integrate the flavors. There should be substantial sauce but if the curry appears too thick, add ¼ cup water and simmer another 2 or 3 minutes. Adjust the salt if necessary.

Serve warm with rice and several vegetarian side dishes.

SERVES 8.

VEGETABLE CURRY WITH FENUGREEK (INDIAN)

Fenugreek, that slightly bitter seed, is quite viscous when ground and used in curries or, as it is used in Calcutta, as a table condiment.

3	tablespoons vegetable oil
1/8	teaspoon black mustard seed
1/4	teaspoon fenugreek seed
2	tablespoons chopped shallot
3	cloves garlic, chopped
3–4	tablespoons hot red chili powder, to taste
2	teaspoons ground coriander
1/2	teaspoon cumin
1	teaspoon turmeric
3	tablespoons water
1/4	cup tamarind paste dissolved in 1 cup water, strained (see How to Make, page 289)
1	large potato (1/2 pound), peeled and cut into 1-inch cubes
1/2	pound carrots, cut into 1/2-inch cubes
3/4	cup diced ripe tomato
1	Oriental eggplant, cut into 1-inch cubes (2 cups)
5	fresh or dried curry leaves (available in Indian, Thai, and Southeast Asian markets)
1 1/2	cups "regular" coconut milk (see page14)
1	teaspoon salt

1. Heat the oil in a large pan and pop the mustard and fenugreek seeds over low heat. Add the shallot and garlic and stir-fry a moment.

2. Make a paste with the chili powder, coriander, cumin, turmeric, and water. Add to the shallot/garlic mixture and stir-fry for 2 minutes. Stir in the tamarind liquid and bring to a boil.

3. Add the potato, carrots, and tomato, cover, and simmer over low heat for 10 minutes to soften the vegetables. Add the eggplant, curry leaves, and coconut milk and simmer for 15 minutes. Adjust the salt. There will be substantial sauce.

Serves with steamed rice.

SERVES 8.

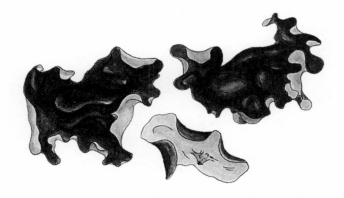

LUMPIAH SABAH (INDIAN)

Vegetarian Spring Rolls

Most people have enjoyed jícama, the white-fleshed and crisp turnip-like vegetable in *rojak,* and other salad-type preparations. In these spring rolls, jícama is part of the cooked stuffing.

The Stuffing

1   *tablespoon vegetable oil*
1   *cup finely shredded cabbage*
1   *carrot, grated*
1   *cup bean sprouts*
1   *cup julienne-sliced jícama (see Glossary)*
½   *teaspoon salt*
¼   *teaspoon pepper*

The Spring Rolls

10   *round spring roll wrappers, 7 inches in diameter*
 1   *egg, beaten*
 2   *cups vegetable oil for deep frying*

1.   Prepare the stuffing: Heat the oil in a wok or large skillet, add all the vegetables, salt, and pepper and stir-fry over moderate heat for 3 to 4 minutes. Strain the mixture through a metal sieve to remove all excess liquid. Set aside.

2.   Prepare the spring rolls: Put 2 generous tablespoons of the stuffing on the bottom part of the wrapper. Roll the wrapper over once firmly, then fold each end over, right then left. Roll the wrapper into a cylinder, then moisten the top edge of the wrapper with the egg. Fold over once more to seal. (Each spring roll will be about 3 inches long and 1 inch thick.)

3.   Heat the oil in a wok until hot and fry the spring rolls, one at a

time, over moderate heat until crisp brown. Drain briefly on paper towels. Keep warm. Be sure to reheat the oil until hot after frying each roll.

Serve warm with chili sauce, tomato ketchup, or other sauces or dips of your choice.

MAKES 10 ROLLS.

BINDE KARI (INDIAN)

Lady Finger Curry

Lady finger is the name given in British colonial countries to the vegetable of the botanical cotton family that we call okra. In Calcutta, when I lived there, okra was known as *bamiya*. In Malaysia, it is called *binde*. This vegetarian curry is a fine marriage of spices, seasonings, and okra.

2	*tablespoons vegetable oil*
1	*medium onion, sliced (1/2 cup)*
1	*teaspoon finely chopped ginger*
1	*clove garlic, chopped fine*
1	*tablespoon hot red chili powder*
1	*teaspoon ground coriander*
1/4	*teaspoon ground cumin*
1/2	*teaspoon turmeric*
1/2	*teaspoon poppy seed, ground*
1/2	*teaspoon salt, or to taste*
1 1/2	*cups water*
1	*tablespoon tamarind paste dissolved in 1/4 cup water, strained (see How to Make, page 289)*
1	*pound whole okra, tops and bottoms slightly trimmed*
1	*ripe medium tomato, cut into 8 wedges*

1. Heat the oil in a large pan, add the onion, and stir-fry over moderate heat until golden brown. Add the ginger, garlic, chili powder, coriander, cumin, turmeric, poppy seed, and salt and stir-fry 2 minutes.

2. Add the water, bring to a boil, and add the tamarind liquid and the okra. Simmer, stirring gently now and then, over low heat for 10 minutes. Stir in the tomato. Adjust the salt if necessary.

    Serve warm with rice.

SERVES 8.

BINDE (NONYA)

Lady Finger Salad

This is a Nonya-style recipe from Malacca, although my teacher, a Nonya, lived in Kuala Lumpur. This salad is for hot, tropical days, of which there is no shortage in Malaysia. (This recipe contains dried shrimp.)

2	*cups water*
1	*pound okra (lady fingers), tops and bottoms trimmed*
1/4	*cup water*
3–4	*fresh hot chilis, to taste, sliced*
1	*teaspoon dried shrimp (available in Asian markets)*
1/2	*teaspoon* belacan, *toasted (see Glossary)*
1	*tablespoon fresh lime juice*
1	*medium onion, sliced thin (1/2 cup)*
1/8	*teaspoon salt*
1/2	*teaspoon sugar*
2	*tablespoons crisp fried shallots (see How to Make, page 288) for garnish*

1. Bring the water to a boil in a large pan, add the okra, and cook over low heat for 3 minutes. Drain.
2. Process the chilis, shrimp, *belacan*, lime juice, onion, salt, and sugar with the water to a smooth sauce.
3. Arrange the okra on a serving platter and pour the sauce over it. Garnish with the fried shallots.

    Serve at room temperature.

SERVES 6 OR 7.

KANGKONG BELACAN (NONYA)

Water Spinach with Belacan

Here is a happy marriage between the long, slender stalks of *kangkong* (water spinach) with its tender leaves, which is available all over tropical Asia and New York's Chinatown, and *belacan,* relatively unknown in the west, one of those seasonings derived from the sea, fermented and preserved. Before using and to enhance its flavor, *belacan* must be toasted lightly for several minutes in the oven or toaster oven as I do. For more information on it, see the Glossary. (This recipe contains dried shrimp.)

3   *shallots, sliced*
3   *cloves garlic, sliced*
2–3 *fresh hot red chilis, to taste, sliced*
2   *teaspoons small dried shrimp (available in Asian markets)*
1/2 *teaspoon* belacan, *toasted*
1   *tablespoon vegetable oil*
1   *pound* kangkong *(water spinach), tender leaves and stems, cut into 2-inch pieces*
1/4 *teaspoon sugar*
2   *tablespoons plus 2 teaspoons water*

1. Process the shallots, garlic, chilis, shrimp, and *belacan* with the 2 tablespoons water to moisten the mixture to a coarse paste.
2. Heat the oil in a wok or skillet and stir-fry the paste over low heat for 2 minutes. Add the *kangkong* and sugar and stir-fry for 2 minutes. Add the 2 teaspoons water and stir-fry 2 minutes more. There will be no sauce.

    Serve warm with rice and other dishes.

SERVES 5 OR 6.

PAKIS BELACAN (ETHNIC PEOPLE)
Wild Jungle Fern Stir-Fry with Belacan

My first taste of the jungle (wild) fern was in Sabah, Borneo, where it was prepared in a quick stir-fry. Generously watered by monsoon rains, the ferns turned up more frequently in Sarawak, as a constant source of fresh greens eaten by the ethnic people. Flavored by *belacan, pakis,* filled with iron and vitamin C, quickly became one of my favorite side dishes.

2   *tablespoons vegetable oil*
4   *shallots, sliced thin*
3   *cloves garlic, sliced thin*
1   *teaspoon finely chopped fresh hot red chili*
½   *teaspoon* belacan, *toasted (see Glossary), dissolved in 1 tablespoon hot water*
1   *pound young jungle fern tops*

> Heat the oil in a wok or skillet, add the shallots, garlic, and chili, and stir-fry over low heat for 2 minutes. Add the *belacan* and fern tops, and stir-fry for 4 minutes more.
>
> Serve warm with rice.

SERVES 4.

NOTE Unless you live in Malaysia, by all means consider a substitute for jungle ferns. I have used watercress, which is excellent, as well as mustard greens and fiddlehead ferns in season. Or use other Chinese green leaf vegetables.

KACANG LENDIR BELACAN

Lady Fingers with Belacan and Vinegar

Okra, as we know it, is known in some countries as lady fingers and in Malaysia as *binde*. Its popularity is unassailable and the flavor and texture equally so. The vinegar adds flavor and is intended to prevent the release of too much viscous liquid from the okra, especially when it is overcooked.

1   *pound okra, tops and bottoms slightly trimmed, then halved crosswise*
1   *tablespoon white vinegar*

Follow the same instructions for Wild Jungle Fern with Belacan (see preceding recipe) but substitute the halved okra, and stir in the vinegar. Cook no longer than 5 minutes.

Serve warm with rice.

SERVES 6.

SAYUR CAMPUR (ETHNIC PEOPLE)

Local Mixed Vegetable Stir-Fry

I observed the local people in the *kampongs* of Sarawak growing baby corn, longbeans, and cucumbers for themselves, and they can go into the fields and gather the wild fern. Others grow rice but not to sell and live an almost self-sufficient life without a telephone or electricity. The twentieth century is on the perimeter of their lives and yet they are comfortable.

1	*tablespoon vegetable oil*
5	*cloves garlic, sliced*
5	*shallots, sliced*
	a ¹/₂-inch piece ginger, sliced thin
10	*fresh or canned whole baby corn*
1	*young cucumber, unpeeled but sliced*
5	*snow peas, or more, if you wish*
1	*cup longbeans, cut into 1-inch pieces*
1	*small carrot, sliced thin diagonally*
1	*cup shredded cabbage*
1	*tablespoon soy sauce*
¹/₄	*teaspoon salt*
¹/₄	*teaspoon pepper*
1	*tablespoon water*

1. Heat the oil in a wok or large skillet, add the garlic first, and stir-fry it for a moment. Add the shallots and ginger and stir-fry over low heat for 1 minute.
2. Add the "veggies"—the corn, cucumber, snow peas, longbeans, carrot, and cabbage—and continue to stir-fry for 2 minutes. Add the soy sauce, salt, pepper, and water and stir-fry for 2 minutes for a crunchy texture and 2 minutes more for a softer crunch.

    Serve warm with rice.

SERVES 4 OR 5.

TIYUNG BELACAN
(ETHNIC PEOPLE, BIDAYUH)

Oriental Eggplant with Belacan

A little bit of *belacan* goes a long way. It has the concentrated flavor of the sea and gives to any dish more dimension. This recipe is from the Bidayuh people in their self-sufficient *kampongs*.

4	*cloves garlic, sliced*
3	*shallots, sliced*
1	*small onion, sliced (¹/₃ cup)*
	a ¹/₄-inch piece ginger, sliced
¹/₂	*teaspoon* belacan, *toasted (see Glossary)*
¹/₂	*teaspoon chopped fresh hot red chili*
2	*tablespoons water*
2	*tablespoons vegetable oil*
1	*pound Oriental eggplant (2), cut into wedges*
¹/₄	*teaspoon salt*
¹/₈	*teaspoon pepper*

1. Process the garlic, shallots, onion, ginger, *belacan,* and chili moistened with the water to a smooth paste.
2. Heat the oil in a wok or large pan, add the garlic paste, and stir-fry it over low heat for 2 minutes.
3. Add the eggplant, salt, and pepper and stir-fry about 4 minutes to soften the eggplant and integrate the flavors.

    Serve warm with rice and meat or fish dishes.

SERVES 4.

Soups

On my many trips to the tropics, I've always checked out the soups on any given menu. Soups can be substantial, and the Malaysian Chinese include noodles, fish cakes and balls, bean sprouts, shrimp, and other seafood, as well as meats, to create a filling and satisfying bowl.

Then there is the hearty oxtail soup of the Malays that is a complete meal, cooked over low heat for several hours with spices and seasonings that turn an odd part of the cow into something quite different.

The Indians have their lentil soups that can also be used to enhance a large bowl of plain cooked rice. A soup of the poor, Rasam (page 202) is a soup of spices and seasonings, without meat broth, completely vegetarian, and as with all foods of this type one never even notices the absence of meat.

One unusual aspect when serving these soups is that they are most generally served at room temperature rather than piping hot. The temperature of the atmosphere in this part of the world is hot enough.

TOM YAM (MALAY)

Spiced Soup with Seafood

Tom yam is related to the Chinese preparation Steamboat (page 186) in this way: The presentation is similar. The soup and ingredients are prepared in the kitchen and served in the same container and in the same way as Steamboat is, over a heating element at the table. Well seasoned with fresh hot green chilis, lemongrass, and garlic but without Chinese ingredients such as tofu and noodles, *tom yam* may, therefore, be considered a Malay family-style soup.

1	*tablespoon corn oil*
2	*cloves garlic, lightly smashed with the flat side of a cleaver*
1	*stalk lemongrass, bottom 5 inches, cracked*
1	*kaffir lime leaf (available in Southeast Asian markets)*
1	*stalk celery, sliced*
8	*cups water*
¹⁄₂	*pound medium shrimp, peeled but tails left on*
¹⁄₂	*pound squid, sliced into rings*
1	*ripe medium tomato, sliced (1 cup)*
2	*small fresh hot green chilis, lightly smashed with the flat side of a cleaver*
2	*whole shallots*
1	*teaspoon salt, or to taste*
2	*tablespoons fresh lime juice*

1. Heat the oil in a wok or pan and brown the garlic over moderate heat for 2 minutes. Add the lemongrass, lime leaf, and celery and stir-fry 1 minute. Then add the water, bring to a boil, and simmer for 5 minutes.

2. Now add the shrimp, squid, tomato, chilis, shallots, and salt and cook the soup over low heat for 15 minutes. Lastly, stir in the lime juice.

   Serve hot with white rice.

SERVES 6 TO 8.

Bubur Lambok (Malay)

Rice Porridge with Fish

This porridge with fish is served on Ramadan in the home of a friend in Terngganu. It is a tasty and satisfying dish, prepared typically Malay style — one of the many rice porridges, some sweet, some not, in the cuisine.

It is ideal for serving on the coldest winter days in temperate climates.

1 *pound mackerel*
1 *cup rice, well rinsed*
2 *cups "regular" coconut milk (see page 14)*
1 *teaspoon black pepper*
2 *scallions, sliced*
1/2 *cup celery leaves, chopped*
1 *stalk lemongrass, bottom 5 inches, cracked*
1 *teaspoon salt, or to taste*

1. Cook the mackerel in 2 cups water over low heat for 8 minutes. Drain. Remove the meat from the bones, discard the bones, and break the meat into pieces. Set aside.
2. Cook the rice in 3 cups boiling water for 10 minutes. Add all the remaining ingredients and the mackerel, cover, simmer over low heat for 1/2 hour.

   Serve warm, with a bowl of crispy *ikan bilis* (see Glossary) and a bowl of roasted peanuts that each diner sprinkles over the porridge.

SERVES 6.

SINGGANG IKAN (MALAY)

Tamarind Fish Soup

This was described to me by my cook as a "famous fish soup" in Terngganu on the east coast of Malaysia, where I was spending some days. The pronounced tamarind flavor with the other seasonings is inspired.

4   *cups water*
    a 1-inch piece galangal (see Glossary), sliced
4   *cloves garlic, sliced*
½   *teaspoon turmeric*
2   *shallots, sliced*
½   *teaspoon salt, or to taste*
1   *teaspoon coriander seed*
¼   *cup tamarind paste dissolved in ½ cup water, strained (see How to Make, page 289)*
2   *pounds whole tuna fish or mackerel, sliced crosswise into 8 pieces*

1. Bring the water to a boil in a pan over low heat. Add all the remaining ingredients, except the fish, and cook for 10 minutes to blend and intensify the flavors.
2. Add the fish and simmer, covered, over low heat for 10 minutes. Adjust the salt if necessary.

    Serve hot with white rice.

SERVES 8

SUP EKOR (MALAY)

Clear Oxtail Soup

Kota Bharu is the capital city of the state of Kelantan; one can expect several good museums and good food there, especially this popular oxtail soup. I was in Kota Bharu during the monsoon season when it rained for five days and nights; it is known for rain, too . . . a good time, I might add, to sample *sup ekor.*

2   *pounds oxtails, cut by the butcher into 8 pieces*
6   *cups water*
1   *medium onion, sliced (½ cup)*
4   *cloves garlic, sliced*
1   *lobe star anise*
     a 1-inch piece cinnamon stick
1   *tablespoon white mustard seed*
2   *cardamom pods*
¼   *teaspoon fennel seed*
1   *teaspoon salt, or to taste*

1.   Cook all the ingredients together in a large pan over low heat, until the oxtails are tender, 2 to 3 hours, adding more water if necessary, should it evaporate too quickly.

      The soup can also be prepared in a pressure cooker; reduce the water to 4 cups and the cooking time by half.

      Note that at the end of the cooking time, whether in a pan or pressure cooker, there should be about 5 cups clear broth.

      Serve hot, meat and broth, with rice.

SERVES 8.

EKOR ASAM PEDAS (MALAY)

Oxtail Soup, Sour and Chili Hot

I tasted this very popular soup in Sabah, Borneo. Hearty and strongly seasoned in the Malay way, it is unexpected in this tropical paradise.

3   *medium onions, sliced (1½ cups)*
10   *cloves garlic, sliced*
   a 2-inch piece ginger, sliced
¼   *cup plus 8 cups water*
2   *tablespoons corn oil*
¼   *cup* chili boh *(see How to Make, page 290)*
½   *teaspoon turmeric*
2   *pounds oxtails, cut by the butcher into 8 to 10 pieces*
4   *stalks lemongrass, bottom 5 inches, cracked*
4   *kaffir lime leaves (available in Southeast Asian markets)*
2   *teaspoons salt*
½   *teaspoon pepper*
10   kemiri *(macadamia nuts), crushed*
⅓   *cup tamarind paste dissolved in ⅔ cup water, strained (see How to Make, page 289)*

1.   Process the onions, garlic, and ginger with the ¼ cup water to a smooth paste.
2.   Heat the oil in a pan and stir-fry the paste, *chili boh*, and turmeric over low heat for 2 minutes, until the aroma rises.
3.   Add the oxtails and brown on all sides for 2 minutes. Add the 8 cups water, lemongrass, lime leaves, salt, pepper, nuts, and tamarind liquid. Bring to a boil and simmer, covered, over low heat for about 1½ hours, or until the oxtail meat is tender.
     (Should you want to use a pressure cooker for this recipe,

use all the same measurements for the spices but reduce the water to 6 cups and cook for 1 hour.)

Serve warm with rice, a pickle, and Ulam Ulam (page 156) as side dishes.

SERVES 8.

Sup Tulang (Malay)

Ribs of Beef Soup

This extravagantly seasoned beef soup is more or less clear and can be served with or without the ribs, in which case they can then be served separately at the same meal or at another time.

6	*shallots, sliced*
5	*cloves garlic, sliced*
	a 2-inch piece ginger, sliced
1/4	*cup plus 4 quarts water*
1/2	*teaspoon cumin seed*
1/2	*teaspoon fennel seed*
1/2	*teaspoon coriander seed*
2	*tablespoons vegetable oil*
	a 2-inch piece cinnamon stick
3	*whole star anise*
4	*whole cloves*
4	*cardamom pods*
4	*pounds beef ribs with some meat*
2	*teaspoons salt, or to taste*
1	*teaspoon black pepper*
2	*scallions, sliced thin, for garnish*
2	*sprigs flat-leaf parsley, chopped, for garnish*

1. Process the shallots, garlic, and ginger with the 1/4 cup water to a paste.
2. Toast the cumin, fennel, and coriander seeds in a dry skillet over low heat for 2 minutes. Then crush or grind.
3. Heat the oil in a large pan. Add the shallot paste and stir-fry over low heat for 1 minute. Add the crushed cumin mixture and stir-fry until fragrant. Now add the cinnamon stick, star anise, cloves, and cardamom pods and stir-fry until coated.
4. Add the 4 quarts water and bring to a boil. Add the beef ribs,

bring to a boil, and skim off the foam that rises. Simmer the soup over low heat for 2 hours, which reduces some of the liquid and tenderizes the meat on the ribs.

5. Season with the salt and pepper. Garnish with the scallions and parsley.

Serve broth and beef ribs warm, with rice.

SERVES 8 OR MORE.

NOTE This soup can be made in a pressure cooker, which will reduce the cooking time to 1 hour. The water should be reduced by half, but all the seasonings measurements remain the same. Nevertheless, I prefer the old-fashioned way, as I do with any traditional ethnic dishes.

STEAMBOAT (CHINESE)

There is no other title for this nationally popular family-style dish. Everyone in Malaysia knows this preparation and they search out restaurants that specialize in its intricate but essentially simple idea. It can be cooked in the home but is principally a restaurant offering. I have tasted (really cooked) it in a number of cities. The best one was on a side street in the old town of Ipoh, a very good one in a large garden restaurant in Kuala Lumpur, and a standard one in Kuching, on the island of Borneo.

Here is how it is done. Round tables that seat from four to ten persons are each furnished with a gas burner serviced by a small gas tank under the table. A round pan is placed on the burner and partially filled with clear chicken or beef broth.

Plates of a wide assortment of ingredients — won tons, prawn dumplings, stuffed bean curd, plain cubed bean curd, baby abalone, sliced venison steak, sliced chicken, tiger prawns in the shell, sliced fish fillet, oysters, black mushrooms, crab, scallops, dried Chinese sausages, and other items, depending upon the price per person (all you can eat costs from $8.00 to $10.00) and the generosity of the restaurant — are then brought to the table.

Of special interest to all are the green vegetables that temper the flavor of the broth and offer a contrast to the high-protein caliber of the other ingredients. Vegetables might include bok choy, *kangkong* (water spinach), watercress, wild ferns, and other local greens so dear to the hearts of the Chinese.

All portions on the individual plates are for as large a variety as you wish to muster, at least eight to ten different items and enough for four persons or more depending on the diners.

Side dishes of soy sauce and a chili-hot dipping sauce with an intriguing hint of *belacan* (see Glossary) are available. There are also thinly sliced green chilis pickled in vinegar and fresh hot red chili slices as side-dish tastings.

1. In a pan bring the broth of your choice to a boil over a burner. Then, according to your personal preference, your assortment of ingredients is put into the broth, a few pieces of each item with a green leaf or two, and left to simmer for 5 minutes or enough to cook through. They are removed from the pan with chopsticks, dipped into a sauce, and eaten. This process goes along casually with the conversation.

2. Some of the broth, which has now been considerably strengthened by the seafood, greens, or meats that have been cooked in it, is ladled into bowls and sipped, sometime with cooked rice added, which I personally prefer.

3. The process repeats itself with a different assortment of foods added to the simmering broth. I have seen individuals in restaurants go up to the refrigerated tables to select more seafood, meats, and greens (all you can eat for $8.00 to $10.00 per person) until they are satiated. It is a genuine bargain and fat free and richly flavored, with a large quantity and wide variety of quality items.

Steamboat can be prepared in the home on your own gas burners by judiciously planning the serving. I suggest that there be two servings, the initial one, let us say for six persons, allowing one cup of broth for each. When the broth boils, add one half of all the ingredients you have decided to include (at least eight different varieties) and simmer them until cooked. Serve with some broth.

The second serving would be the balance of the ingredients. All items and broth should be eaten with side dishes of steamed white rice, dipping sauces, and hot chilis.

Noodle Soup with Assorted Garnishes (Chinese)

This is a traditional soup that is sold in hole-in-the-wall restaurants ($0.80 per bowl) all day and after dark when the street food carts emerge from their daytime siesta in Malacca. It is so pervasive and reliable that I wondered why anyone cooked at home.

The following assortment of ingredients is added to a clear, simply seasoned broth. The soup is filling, nourishing, and easy to assemble.

4   *cups homemade chicken or pork broth*
4   *fish balls, one for each person (see Note)*
1   *firm or soft square tofu, cut into 1-inch cubes*
    okra stuffed with fish paste (see page 127, Note)
    fresh green semi-hot chilis stuffed with fish paste (see Note)
    bitter melon slices stuffed with fish paste (see Note)
    bean sprouts
    any assortment of Chinese greens, such as bok choy, sliced
    cooked rice noodles, narrow or wide style
    cooked egg noodles, as a substitute for rice noodles
    fresh hot red chilis, seeded and sliced thin, for garnish

scallions, sliced thin, for garnish
fresh coriander leaves, for garnish

Bring the broth to a boil in a pan. Select 5 or more different in-gredients, plus noodles. Put a generous amount of noodles in the bowl, sprinkle your choice of garnishes over the noodles, and pour the hot broth over all.

Serve hot.

SERVES 4.

NOTE Fish balls can be prepared at home (page 192) or purchased in Chinese groceries.

The stuffed okra, chilis, and bitter melon are to be steamed over hot water for 10 minutes before being added to the soup.

HOKKIEN MEE (CHINESE)

Shrimp and Noodle Soup

The Hokkien are a community of Chinese that came to Malaysia centuries ago from China. They have produced what is, in my opinion, the most satisfying of all egg noodle soups. With the emphasis on shrimp, it has among its ingredients the shells of peeled shrimp, two pounds if available, that can be saved in advance and frozen until ready to use.

2	*tablespoons vegetable oil*
6	*shallots, sliced*
1	*to 2 pounds shrimp shells, well rinsed*
1	*tablespoon* chili boh *(see How to Make, page 290)*
2	*pounds chicken bones, including backs and legs*
3–4	*red dried hot chilis to taste*
4	*quarts water*
1	*teaspoon salt, or to taste*
2	*tablespoons rock sugar or 1 tablespoon white sugar*
1	*pound egg noodles, blanched in boiling water for 2 minutes and drained*
2	*cups beans sprouts, blanched in boiling water 1 minute and drained*
1	*cup sliced cooked boneless chicken*
1	*pound cooked peeled and deveined medium shrimp*
1/3	*cup crisp fried shallots (see How to Make, page 288)*
2	*hard-cooked eggs, quartered*

1. Heat the oil in a wok or large skillet. Add the shallots and shrimp shells and stir-fry over low heat for 5 minutes. Add the *chili boh*, chicken bones, dried chilis, and water and bring to a boil. Add the salt and sugar and simmer over low heat for 1 hour, which should reduce the liquid by half. Strain the liquid and discard the shells, bones, and other solids. Now you have a strong Hokkien broth.

2. To serve, put a portion of the egg noodles in Chinese soup

bowls. Garnish with 1 heaping tablespoon each of bean sprouts, chicken, and shrimp, 1 teaspoon crisp shallots, and 1 egg wedge. Pour in about 1 cup of the hot Hokkien broth. Extra broth may be frozen for future use.

Serve hot.

SERVES 8.

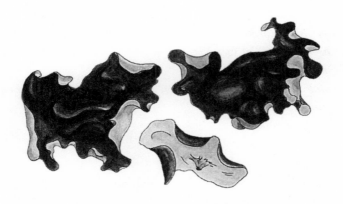

Hock Chew (Chinese)

Fish Ball Soup

He was introduced as the best fish ball maker in Penang—a little brown, wrinkled, toothless sweet old man with a substantial vocabulary of English. He was a retired hawker. How many years can one push the food cart from one food court to another?

Fish Balls

1¼   *pounds flounder fillets or any white fish, sliced*
½   *cup tapioca (cassava) flour*
¾–1 *cup water*
2   *teaspoons salt*
6   *cups chicken broth*
½   *teaspoon garlic oil (see Note)*
⅛   *teaspoon white pepper*
¼   *pound thin rice noodles* (bihun), *soaked in water 10 minutes and drained*
     Soy sauce to taste
2   *scallions, green part only, sliced*

1. Prepare the fish balls: Process the fish, flour, water, and salt to a smooth paste using enough water to make a smooth, firm consistency.

2. Bring a large pan of water to a rapid rolling boil.

3. Scoop 1 tablespoon of the fish paste and roll in the palm of your hand moistened with cold water into a ball 1 inch in diameter. Drop the balls, one by one, into the boiling water and cook for 1 minute. Remove with a slotted spoon. Set aside.

4. Bring the broth with the garlic oil and pepper to a boil over low heat.

5. To serve, fill each Chinese soup bowl with 2 to 3 tablespoons of the softened noodles, 2 fish balls, ¼ teaspoon soy

sauce, and a teaspoon of scallion. Ladle in about 1 cup of the hot broth.

Serve hot.

SERVES 6.

NOTE Garlic oil is the oil that results after you fry garlic (or shallot) slices to be used as garnishes until crisp. The oil is very flavorful.

Penang Asam Laksa (Chinese)

Penang Fish and Noodle Soup

This famous soup is known throughout Malaysia and justifiably so, since it is generous with its seasonings, fish, and tamarind, among other ingredients. The competition from Kuching, Sarawak, is very strong since there they refer to their famous *laksa*, which is a breakfast food and found all over the city in several grades—regular and superior. One acquaintance in Kuching told me that he could not start the day without his bowl of *laksa*. The following is the Penang version.

 a 1-inch piece galangal (*see Glossary*), cracked
4 stalks lemongrass, bottom 5 inches, white part only, cracked
7 cups water
2 pounds (4) small whole mackerel, cooked in 4 cups boiling water for 15 minutes, fish and broth reserved, bones discarded
4 fresh hot red chilis, sliced
4 dried red chilis, seeded
5 shallots, sliced
4 cloves garlic, sliced
½ teaspoon turmeric
1 teaspoon belacan, toasted (*see Glossary*)
½ teaspoon salt, or to taste
1 tablespoon petis (*see Glossary*)
¼ cup tamarind paste dissolved in ½ cup water, strained (*see How to Make, page 289*)
1 pound rice noodles, ¼ inch wide, blanched in boiling water for 1 minute
1 cup cubed peeled ripe pineapple (½-inch cubes)
2 young cucumbers, unpeeled, cut into ½-inch cubes
⅓ cup mint leaves
1 small onion, sliced in the round (⅓ cup)
1 wild ginger bud (bunga kantan), sliced (optional, *see Glossary*)

1. Put the galangal, lemongrass, and 7 cups water in a pan with the reserved mackerel stock and bring to a boil.

2. Process in a blender or food processor the fresh chilis, dried chilis, shallots, garlic, turmeric, *belacan,* salt, *petis,* and tamarind liquid to a smooth paste. Add the paste to the pan and simmer the mixture over low heat for 1 hour. Add the mackerel pieces, cut into cubes.

3. To serve, put a portion of the rice noodles into each Chinese soup bowl. Garnish with pieces of pineapple and cucumber, the mint leaves, onion rings, and the wild ginger bud, if using. Ladle hot, spiced broth with pieces of fish over all.

    Serve hot.

SERVES 8 OR MORE.

KOAY TEOW THING (CHINESE)

Rice Noodle Soup with Meats

Here is another of those extraordinary hawker soups of Penang that is filling, flavorful, fragrant, and fastidious with its assortment of spices and seasonings. Hawker food is labor intensive and à la carte, and has ingredients that take advantage of land and sea.

10   *cups water*
     a 4-pound whole chicken, loose skin and fat discarded
½   *pound boneless pork*
1   *pound pork bones*
1   *teaspoon rock sugar or white sugar*
1   *teaspoon salt, or to taste*
1   *pound rice noodles, ¼ inch wide*
2   *fish balls (per person) (page 192, and see Note)*
1   *cup thin sliced ground fish loaf (allow 2 slices per serving, see Note)*
¼   *teaspoon garlic oil (see Note page 193) with garlic (per person)*
¼   *teaspoon oyster sauce (per person)*
¼   *teaspoon soy sauce (per person)*
2   *scallions, green part only, sliced thin*
2   *fresh hot red chilis, sliced thin*

1.   Bring 10 cups water (or enough to cover the chicken) to a boil in a large pan and add the chicken, pork, and pork bones. Bring to a boil and skim off the foam that rises. Add the rock sugar and salt, and simmer over low heat for 45 minutes, enough to cook the chicken and pork.

2.   Remove the chicken, pork, and bones. Discard the bones. Cool and cut the chicken and pork into thin slices. Set aside.

3.   Bring another pan of water to a boil, add the rice noodles, and cook for 1 minute. Drain immediately. Set aside.

4.   To serve, put about ½ cup noodles in a bowl. Top with several slices of chicken and pork. Add the fish balls, fish loaf slices,

garlic oil with garlic, and oyster and soy sauce. Add several scallion slices and red chili slices to taste. Pour ¾ cup soup over the ingredients.

Serve hot.

SERVES 8.

NOTE Fish balls as well as ground fish loaf may be purchased in Chinese groceries.

Sup Masak Ayam Lemak (Hakka Chinese)

Winter Melon Soup with Chicken

Winter melon soup is reliable; everyone likes it. The large green melon, lightly dusted with white powdered wax when mature, can be purchased in Chinatown, cut to order. The seasonings here are Chinese, of the Hakka community.

1   *pound winter melon, peeled and cut into little finger-sized spears*
3   *cups water*
1   *ripe tomato, coarsely cut (1 cup)*
4   *cloves garlic, sliced*
3   *shallots, sliced*
    a ¹/₂-inch piece ginger, sliced
¹/₄ *cup water*
1   *teaspoon vegetable oil*
1   *cup "regular" coconut milk (see page 14)*
1   *cup cubed boneless chicken breast (1-inch cubes)*
1   *teaspoon salt*
¹/₄ *teaspoon pepper*
¹/₂ *teaspoon hot red chili powder*
¹/₂ *teaspoon sugar*
1   *stalk lemongrass, bottom 5 inches, cut into 6 pieces, cracked
    (see Note)*
2   *kaffir lime leaves (available at Southeast Asian markets)*
¹/₂ *cup fresh coriander leaves and stems, sliced*

1.   Put the winter melon into a pan with the water, bring to a boil, cover, and simmer over low heat for ¹/₂ hour. (The melon is very firm and will take time to soften.) Add the tomato and continue to cook for another ¹/₂ hour, or until the melon is soft and translucent.

2. Process the garlic, shallots, and ginger with the water to a smooth paste.

3. Heat the oil in a nonstick skillet and stir-fry the spice paste over low heat for 2 minutes. Add the coconut milk, chicken, salt, pepper, sugar, chili powder, lemongrass, and lime leaves and simmer for 10 minutes.

4. Add the chicken mixture to the pan with the winter melon soup. Simmer the soup over low heat for 15 minutes. Adjust the salt, sugar, and chili powder, if more is wanted. Lastly, stir in the coriander leaves, and simmer 1 minute more.

Serve warm with rice.

SERVES 6.

NOTE Lemongrass is often too firm to crack with anything but a hammer. Tap each piece firmly 2 or 3 times to release the flavor before adding to the soup.

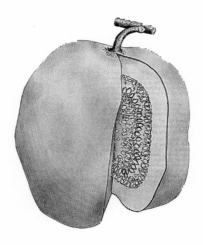

Laksa (Chinese)
Ten Thousand Mixture Soup

There is a certain mystique about the virtues of *laksa*, and there are many. The *laksa* of Penang is not like that of Kuching, Sarawak. It is they in Kuching who pride themselves on the *laksa* to end all others. There are many eating houses in Kuching (which means "cat") that feature their version of *laksa* from about $0.80 on up to $1.20, which seems extravagant but isn't. I tried several of them over a week's breakfasts, which is when it is traditionally eaten. The recipe that follows is the best in my opinion.

Gravy

6 *shallots, sliced*
6 *cloves garlic, sliced*
3 *fresh hot red chilis, seeded and sliced*
3 *stalks lemongrass, the bottom 3 inches, and the heart, sliced*
1 *whole star anise*
   a 1-inch piece cinnamon stick
4 *cardamom pods*
2 *whole cloves*
5 *cups water*
3 *tablespoons corn oil*
2 *cups "regular" coconut milk (see page 14)*
2 *teaspoons salt, or to taste*

The Laksa

1 *pound cooked small shrimp, peeled and deveined*
1 *cup cooked shredded chicken*
½ *pound* bihun *(thin rice noodles), soaked in water 15 minutes and drained*
2 *cups bean sprouts, blanched in hot water 2 minutes and drained*

a 2-egg fried omelette, cooled and shredded

¼ cup crisp fried shallots (see How to Make, page 288), for garnish

2 scallions, sliced thin, for garnish

1. Prepare the gravy: Process the shallots, garlic, chilis, lemon-grass, star anise, cinnamon, cardamom pods, and cloves with ¼ cup of the water into a smooth paste.

2. Heat the oil in a large pan and stir-fry the paste over low heat for about 3 minutes to develop a light brown color.

3. Add the balance of the water and bring to a boil. Add the coconut milk and salt and simmer over low heat for 10 minutes. The gravy is now ready to use.

4. Add the shrimp, chicken, rice noodles, bean sprouts, and omelette to the hot gravy. Portion out the *laksa* in individual soup bowls and garnish with the crisp shallots and scallions.

Serve warm.

SERVES 8.

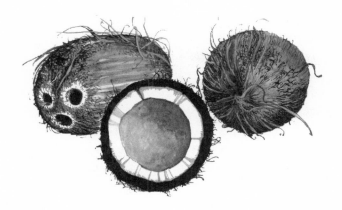

RASAM (INDIAN)

Indian Soup

The soup is completely vegetarian and has considerable verve. Non-Indians refer to this as "Indian soup" and appreciate the battery of tongue-tingling spices.

1	*tablespoon corn oil*
1/4	*teaspoon mustard seed*
1/4	*teaspoon fenugreek seed*
1	*shallot, sliced*
2	*hot red dried chilis*
1/8	*teaspoon asafetida* (hing, *see Glossary*)
6	*fresh or dried curry leaves (available at Indian, Thai, or Southeast Asian markets)*
1	*teaspoon fennel seed*
1	*teaspoon cumin seed*
1	*tablespoon coriander seed*
2	*teaspoons black peppercorns*
8	*cups water*
2	*tablespoons tamarind paste dissolved in 1/2 cup water, strained (see How to Make, page 289)*
4	*cloves garlic, smashed with the flat side of a cleaver*
1	*teaspoon salt, or to taste*
1	*ripe medium tomato, chopped (2/3 cup)*
1/2	*teaspoon turmeric*

1. Heat the oil in a pan and pop the mustard seed over low heat. Add the fenugreek, shallot, chilis, asafetida, and curry leaves and stir-fry a moment.
2. Coarsely crush the fennel, cumin, coriander, and peppercorns and add them to the fried seasonings. Add the water, tamarind liquid, garlic, salt, tomato, and turmeric and simmer over low heat for 10 minutes. Strain the soup through a metal sieve.
   Serve warm.

SERVES 6 OR MORE.

NOTE Some cooks save the spices in the sieve and renew the soup by
    adding more water and reheating it. This is merely an act of economy;
    the soup does not have the bite of the original making.

APPETIZERS AND SNACKS

The first time I tasted Curry Puffs (page 214) in Singapore and at a bus stop snack shop near Ipoh in Malaysia, I was hooked. Then I tasted Penang Popiah (Spring Rolls, page 224) and others, and it occurred to me that one could prepare a number of appetizer-snacks and with a bowl of rice enjoy an eclectic lunch home-style. Since then, a number of the snack-type recipes that follow have entered my personal repertoire. Some can be frozen, such as the Samosas (page 218), then be removed an hour before they are needed and reheated briefly in the oven.

Ethnic appetizers, judiciously selected and prepared, can enrich your diet and entice your guests. They should always be available.

TEMPEYEK (MALAY)

Crisp Crackers with Peanuts

These intriguing snacks have a variety of flavors plus peanuts (called groundnuts) and *ikan bilis* (crisp fried baby anchovies).

½ cup rice flour
½ cup wheat (all-purpose) flour
¼ teaspoon salt
¼ teaspoon chili powder
½ cup water
1 egg, beaten
1 cup corn or your favorite oil for deep frying
2 tablespoons roasted peanuts
2 tablespoons ikan bilis *(crisp fried whole anchovies)*

1. Mix the two flours, salt, chili powder, and water into a smooth batter. Add the egg and mix well.
2. Heat the oil in a wok over moderate heat. Dip a metal ladle or large kitchen spoon into the hot oil. Remove it and fill with the batter. Sprinkle 1 teaspoon peanuts and 3 or 4 anchovies over the top.
3. Submerge the ladle with the batter back into the oil and fry for 1 minute. When ready, the cracker can be loosened from the ladle with a chopstick and can be slid into the oil. Turn it over and lightly brown the other side. Remove with a slotted spoon and drain on paper towels. Make crackers with the remaining batter and drain them in the same manner.

   Serve at room temperature, as a snack with drinks or tea or coffee.

MAKES 6 OR 7 CRACKERS.

Akak Berlauk (Malay)

Stuffed Meat Cakes

Here is another recipe from the Sultan of Kelantan's kitchen as I observed it being made in the shed/kitchen that had elements of both the eighteenth and twentieth century. It was a crosscultural manifestation of the new and the old Malaysia.

The Stuffing

1   tablespoon vegetable oil
    a 1-inch piece ginger, crushed
2   cloves garlic, smashed with the flat side of a cleaver
1   medium onion, chopped (½ cup)
3   tablespoons curry powder
    one 3-pound chicken, cut into 8 pieces, loose skin and fat discarded, or 2 pounds lean ground beef
½   teaspoon gula Malacca (see Glossary)
¼   teaspoon salt
3   cups "regular" coconut milk (see page 14)
1   recipe Akak batter (see page 268)

1. Prepare the stuffing: Heat the oil in a skillet, add the ginger, garlic, and onion, and stir-fry over low heat until the onion is golden. Add the curry powder and chicken pieces and stir-fry for 5 minutes.

2. Add the *gula Malacca*, salt, and coconut milk, bring to a boil, and simmer over low heat until the liquid has completely evaporated. Cool well and remove the meat from the chicken bones. Chop fine.

    If you are using beef, prepare it in the same way but use 2 cups instead of 3 cups coconut milk. Cook the curried stuffing until dry.

3. To make the stuffed cakes: Half fill lightly oiled cupcake tins

with Akak batter. Top with a heaping teaspoon of either the
chicken or ground beef stuffing and cover with more batter.

4. Bake in a preheated 325-degree oven for 5 minutes, or until
    lightly heated.

    Best served warm, or at room temperature.

MAKES ABOUT 30 CUPCAKES.

Rojak (All Malaysia)

Assorted Fruits with Peanut Sauce

This is probably the most popular salad snack in Malaysia, especially on very hot tropical days. It is essentially prepared with tart, firm fruit, cut into random pieces. *Rojak* is flexible. One can include as many tropical fruits and some vegetables as are seasonally available, with the desired amount of sweetness.

The sauce is mixed with a unique seasoning called *petis udan*. It is prepared with prawns (shrimp), sugar, flour, and salt and can be purchased in Chinese groceries. This particular recipe originated with the Chinese cooks of Ipoh.

The Fruit

1   *cup assorted fruits and vegetables cut into 1-inch cubes, for each diner:*
    jícama (see Glossary)
    green mango, peeled
    tart firm apple
    starfruit (carambola)
    young cucumber, unpeeled
    fresh pineapple
    green guava, peeled

The Sauce

1/2   *cup sugar*
2   *tablespoons black soy sauce* (kicip *in Malay, see Glossary)*
2   *tablespoons regular soy sauce*
1/3   *cup* petis *(shrimp paste)*
1   *teaspoon* belacan, *toasted (see Glossary)*
1/4   *cup hot water*
2   *tablespoons coarsely ground peanuts*

Prepare the sauce: Process all the sauce ingredients together, except the peanuts, into a relatively smooth paste. Stir in the peanuts. If the sauce is too thick, add another tablespoon or two of hot water.

To serve, the sauce may be mixed with the fruit in the kitchen or, as is frequently done, served separately. Each diner will serve him- or herself.

Sometimes, the sauce is poured in on the side of the bowl rather than over the *rojak*. Diners then dip each piece into the sauce.

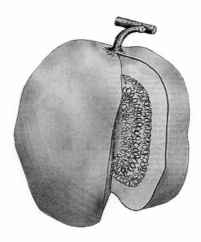

Oo Koay (Chinese)

Penang Yam Cake

This snack is not made with the supermarket yam as we know it, but the rough-skinned whitish-fleshed Asian yam that is always available in Chinatown. I discovered this dish at a hawker stall that was owned by a Hokkien Chinese who served only this, his specialty. The cart opened at 12:30 P.M., and by 6:30 P.M. he and his wife had sold out their entire production. So they packed up the moveable cart stall and pushed it home, a 30-minute job through the streets.

⅓	cup vegetable oil
4	pounds Asian yam, peeled and sliced ¼ inch thick
1	pound rice flour
1	teaspoon salt
1	teaspoon sugar
½	cup crisp fried shallots (see How to Make, page 288)
½	cup small dried shrimp (available at Asian markets), rinsed in warm water and drained
2–3	fresh hot red chilis, thinly sliced
¼	cup hot chili paste (page 144), mixed with tomato ketchup, if desired, to dilute the heat

1. Heat the oil in a wok or large skillet and stir-fry the yam slices over moderate heat until soft, about 8 minutes. Cool and mash coarsely.

2. Mix the mashed yam well with the rice flour, salt, and sugar.

3. Pour the mixture into a lightly oiled round cake pan, about 8 inches in diameter. (The mixture should be about 2 inches high.) Steam the cake, covered, over boiling water for 1 hour, replenishing the water in the wok when needed. To test for doneness, plunge a chopstick into the cake. If it is sticky when removed, then steam it longer, until the chopstick comes out dry.

4.   To serve, cut the cake into 1-inch chunks. Put about ⅔ cup on a plate, sprinkle with the shallots and shrimp, add a few slices of chili, and drizzle the chili paste mixture over all to taste.

Serve as a snack at room temperature anytime.

SERVES 8.

Nargisi Kofta (Indian)

Hidden Quail Eggs

The original method of preparing these delectable appetizers was with hard-cooked chicken eggs. I discovered that the much smaller quail egg with its typical understated flavor makes for a much more interesting way of doing *nargisi kofta*.

1	*pound ground fat-free chicken breast*
2	*tablespoons chopped fresh coriander leaves*
2	*fresh hot green chilis, seeded and chopped*
1/8	*teaspoon white pepper*
1/4	*teaspoon garam masala (see How to Make, page 295)*
1	*teaspoon salt, or to taste*
30	*fresh quail eggs, hard cooked, or canned eggs, drained and rinsed*
	corn oil for baking and/or deep frying

1. Mix together the chicken, coriander, chilis, pepper, garam masala, and salt. Cover each egg with about a 1/2-inch layer of the chicken mixture.

2. Rub a baking pan with 1 tablespoon oil, put the coated eggs in the pan, and bake in a preheated 325-degree oven for 15 minutes. Remove and serve warm as appetizers with your favorite Malaysian dipping sauce.

   Or, heat enough oil for deep frying until hot in a wok and brown the eggs over moderate heat for 2 to 3 minutes. Remove to paper towels to drain.

MAKES ABOUT 30 COVERED QUAIL EGGS.

VEGETABLE PAKORA (INDIAN)

Mashed Deep-Fried Vegetable Snacks

A "local" recipe from the environs of Kuala Lumpur. Cooked vegetables are mashed by hand (not in a processor) so that flecks of color remain, then are rolled into balls and deep fried.

1	*potato (about 6 ounces), peeled and cubed*
1	*cup cauliflower florets*
1	*cup sliced carrot*
1	*cup broccoli florets*
2	*fresh hot green chilis, seeded and chopped*
1	*fresh hot red chili, seeded and chopped*
1/8	*teaspoon ground black pepper*
1	*teaspoon salt, or to taste*
1	*cup* besan *(chick pea flour)*
5	*fresh or dried curry leaves (available at Indian, Thai, or Southeast Asian markets), chopped*
2	*cups corn oil for deep frying*

1. Cook the potato, cauliflower, carrot, and broccoli separately in boiling water with a dash of salt until soft. Drain and mash by hand.
2. Then mix all the mashed vegetables together with the *besan* and curry leaves. (There should be enough moisture in the vegetables so that no additional water need be added to hold the mash together). Shape balls, 1 inch in diameter.
3. Heat enough oil for deep frying until hot in a wok over moderate heat. Brown the snacks in batches, and remove with a slotted spoon to drain briefly on paper towels. These can be cooled, then frozen in plastic containers. Reheat in a preheated 350-degree oven until warmed through.

   Serve warm, as a snack with drinks or tea or coffee.

MAKES ABOUT 12 BALLS.

CURRY PUFFS (INDIAN)

These are one of the most popular snacks in Malaysia, and I have sampled many, in different towns, especially at bus stops when I've been traveling through the countryside.

The Dough

3   cups flour
1/2 teaspoon salt
1   cup water, plus

The Stuffing

2   tablespoons corn oil
1   medium onion, chopped (1/2 cup)
2   potatoes (1/2 pound), peeled and cut into 1/4-inch cubes
1   cup small shrimp, peeled, deveined, and halved lengthwise
1/2 teaspoon ground fennel
1/4 teaspoon ground cinnamon
1   teaspoon hot red chili powder
1/2 teaspoon salt, or to taste
2/3 cup water

1. Prepare the dough: Mix the flour and the salt together, then add water, a little at a time up to 1 cup, to prepare a firm dough. Knead until smooth. (You may need a little bit of additional water; add it sparingly.) Dust with flour, if necessary. Put the dough in a plastic bag and refrigerate for 1 hour.

2. Prepare the stuffing: Heat the oil in a skillet, add the onion, and stir-fry it over low heat for 1 minute. Add all the remaining ingredients, except the water, and stir-fry for 2 minutes.

3.   Add the water, cover the pan, and cook until all the liquid has evaporated and the potatoes are soft. Stir rapidly to break down the stuffing. Cool well. Set aside.

4.   Break off a walnut-sized piece of the dough and roll it out on a well-floured board into a 4-inch circle. Put 1 tablespoon of the stuffing on the bottom half of the dough and moisten the edge of the circle with a little water. Fold the dough over into a half moon and seal the edges with the tines of a fork. Repeat with all the remaining stuffing and dough.

5.   There are two ways to cook the puffs. The first, which I prefer, is to put them on an oiled cookie sheet and bake in a preheated 350-degree oven for about ½ hour, until light brown.

   The other method, which is more common, is to deep fry them, a few at a time, in oil in a wok over moderate heat for about 3 minutes. Remove with a slotted spoon. Drain on paper towels.

   Serve warm.

MAKES ABOUT 20 CURRY PUFFS.

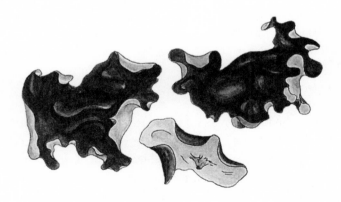

Vegetable Pakora (Indian)

Deep-Fried Vegetable Snacks

A very Indian snack, which my cook in Calcutta, India, during a longtime residence there made in the style of that city. These *pakora* are "local" snacks, made in the style of Kuala Lumpur, the capital of Malaysia. Note that every Indian household has its own combination of spices and vegetables for this preparation.

The Batter

½   *cup water*
1   *teaspoon salt*
1   *cup* besan *(chick pea flour)*
¼   *teaspoon garam masala (see How to Make, page 295)*
¼   *teaspoon white pepper*

The Vegetables

thin diagonal carrot slices
whole small okra
individual spinach leaves
small cauliflower florets

1½ *cups vegetable oil for deep frying*

1. Prepare the batter: Mix all the batter ingredients together in the order in which they are listed. Mix well and let stand ½ hour.
2. Heat the oil in a wok over moderate heat. Dip each vegetable piece by piece into the batter and fry in the oil until brown. The spinach leaves, in particular, are best dipped and fried one at a time. Drain the vegetables briefly on paper towels.
   Serve warm.

MAKES ABOUT 20 PIECES.

Apom Jala (Indian)

Fisherman's Net Pancakes

There is a small metal cup balanced on five legs, each tapered leg with a hole in it one-eighth inch in diameter. I have called it a "jala container," since it is used to make fisherman's net pancakes. If you are interested in a jala container, look for it in Indian markets, where they are modestly priced.

2 *cups flour*
1/2 *teaspoon salt*
1 *egg, beaten*
3–3 1/2 *cups water*
  Several teaspoons butter or margarine, softened

1. Mix the flour, salt, and egg together, adding enough water to produce a batter that is not too thick as it will not dribble through the holes in the jala container. A texture like maple syrup is what is needed.
2. Heat a very lightly oiled nonstick skillet over low heat. Hold the jala container over the pan and pour 1/2 cup of the batter into it. Move the jala container in concentric circles about 7 inches in diameter quickly over the pan as the batter drizzles out. There will be many openings, like a net.
3. Fry 2 minutes, drop 1/4 teaspoon butter or margarine onto the net, and turn it over with a spatula. Brown for 1 minute.

   Remove the net and fold it over in half. Reserve. Make pancakes with the remaining batter in the same manner.

   Serve the nets warm, with curries.

MAKES ABOUT 10 TO 12 NETS.

SAMOSAS (INDIAN)

Meat- or Vegetable-Stuffed Half Moons

The traditional shape of samosas is the half moon, that is to say a round is rolled out, a stuffing is placed on top, and the round is folded over. The following recipes are for two different stuffings, which offers more variety.

Vegetable Stuffing

1   *tablespoon corn oil*
1   *medium onion, sliced thin (¹/₂ cup)*
1   *clove garlic, smashed*
     a ¹/₂-inch piece ginger, sliced and smashed with the flat side of a cleaver
1   *teaspoon hot red chili powder*
1   *teaspoon ground coriander*
¹/₂   *teaspoon ground cumin*
¹/₂   *teaspoon turmeric*
1   *teaspoon salt, or to taste*
1   *medium potato, peeled, cooked, and mashed (²/₃ cup)*
1   *large carrot, peeled, sliced, cooked, and mashed (¹/₂ cup)*
¹/₄   *cup green peas*
1   *cup shredded cabbage*
¹/₄   *cup water*

1.   Heat the oil in a skillet, add the onion, and stir-fry it until golden brown. Add the garlic and ginger, stir a moment, and add the chili powder, coriander, cumin, turmeric, and salt. Mix well.
2.   Add the mashed potato and carrot, green peas, cabbage, and water and stir-fry the mixture over low heat until dry, about 5 minutes. Cool and set aside.

Meat Stuffing

1   *tablespoon corn oil*
½   *teaspoon finely chopped ginger*
1   *clove finely chopped garlic*
½   *pound ground chicken, lean beef, or lamb*
¼   *cup water*
½   *teaspoon salt*
½   *teaspoon ground cumin*
¼   *teaspoon ground fennel*
½   *teaspoon ground coriander*
½   *teaspoon turmeric*
¼   *teaspoon garam masala (see How to Make, page 295)*

1. Heat the oil in a wok or skillet, add the ginger and garlic, and stir rapidly for a moment over low heat. Add the meat and stir-fry another moment until it changes color. Add the water and salt and simmer over low heat until the liquid has evaporated.
2. Add the cumin, fennel, coriander, turmeric, and garam masala and stir-fry until the mixture is dry. Cool well.
3. Prepare the samosas: The wrappers for the half moons are round Shanghai egg roll wrappers. They can be purchased in Chinese groceries. In order to use them they should be trimmed, filled, then folded over into half moons.

   Also, another convenient method is the use of filo pastry sheets that can be purchased in boxes in Middle East groceries and are 12 × 17 inches each. I use filo sheets to prepare triangular samosas this way: Cut the sheets in half to 6 inches wide by 8 inches long. Then fold them lengthwise to make 3-inch-wide strips, with a double thickness.

   Make the triangles: Put 1 heaping teaspoon of the filling of choice on the lower lefthand side of the filo strip. Fold this corner over and to the right to shape a triangle. Then fold this over to the left and continue until the dough is used. Seal the end by brushing the dough with a mixture of 1 teaspoon cornstarch dissolved in 2 tablespoons cold water and pressing it firmly.

Deep fry the half-moons or triangles over moderate heat until light brown, about $^1\!/_2$ minute or less. Drain on paper towels. Serve warm.

MAKES ABOUT 20 HALF MOONS OR TRIANGLES.

KUIH KACANG HIJAU (INDIAN)

Green Mung Bean Snacks

The use of green mung beans in these patties, the same ones that are used for growing bean sprouts, is unexpected. Yet they are filled with protein, have a melting bean character, and are very tasty with drinks.

1/2 cup rice flour

1/4 cup wheat (all-purpose) flour, plus additional for dredging the patties

1/4 teaspoon turmeric

1 cup green mung beans (available in Asian markets), well rinsed

3 cups water

3 tablespoons grated unsweetened dessicated coconut

1 tablespoon sugar

1/4 teaspoon salt

1 egg, beaten

1/2 cup corn oil for pan frying

1. Mix the rice and wheat flours and turmeric together. Set aside.

2. Cook the mung beans in the water over low heat for about 1/2 hour, enough to soften them, and evaporate the liquid.

3. Stir in the coconut, sugar, salt, and egg and combine to form a dough. Shape patties 1/2 inch thick and 2 1/2 inches in diameter. Dredge the patties well in flour to coat all sides.

4. Heat the oil in a skillet and fry the patties over low heat, a few at a time, until brown. Drain on paper towels.

   Serve at room temperature as a snack.

MAKES 10 TO 12 PATTIES.

CUCUR RODE (INDIAN MUSLIM)

Vegetarian Snacks

I met several Indian Muslim ladies who were instrumental in guiding me through a handful of traditional local recipes in Kuching, Sarawak. The family who showed us this combination did not infuse their cooking with hot chili or a catalogue of spices. Moderation was the philosophy for these vegetarian snacks.

3½ *cups flour*
½ *teaspoon salt, or to taste*
½ *teaspoon turmeric*
¼ *teaspoon pepper*
½ *teaspoon hot red chili powder*
1 *teaspoon baking soda*
2 *cups fresh bean sprouts*
1 *cup thinly sliced longbeans, blanched in boiling water 1 minute and drained*
2 *cups water, or more*
1 *cup corn oil for deep frying*

1. Stir all the dry ingredients together, then add the 2 vegetables, mixing well.
2. Add the water, a little at a time, until you have developed a firm dough that can be handled. Shape balls, 1½ inches in diameter, with the dough and set aside.
3. Heat the oil in a wok over moderate heat. Drop the balls, one by one, into the oil and fry them until light brown all over, about 3 to 4 minutes. Remove and drain on paper towels.

    Serve warm sliced or at room temperature with a dip of your own choice.

MAKES 30 BALLS.

VARIATION These may also be prepared as patties. Press each ball down into a patty about ½ inch thick. Pan fry or deep fry until brown on each side, about 3 minutes. Drain on paper towels and serve warm as a snack with either tea or coffee.

PENANG POPIAH (INDIAN MUSLIM)

Spring Rolls

Hawker's stalls in cities are more often than not massed in groups on a side street or collected in food courts where there may be dozens serving different dishes cooked à la carte. Their offerings have become a way of life for the public, where variety and very reasonable prices are a buyer's inducement. The hawkers earn a living in their labor-intensive occupation.

8   *Shanghai egg roll skins, 6 to 7 inches in diameter*
1/2   *cup bottled sweet bean paste*
1   *cup bean sprouts, blanched 1 minute in hot water*
1/2   *pound potato, shredded and blanched in boiling water 3 minutes with 1/2 teaspoon turmeric and 1 teaspoon salt*
2   *soft tofu squares, mashed*
1/2   *cup small shrimp, cooked, peeled, and cut into 1/4-inch pieces*
1/2   *cup crisp fried shallots (see How to Make, page 288)*

1. Spread the egg roll skins out flat on a surface. Spread 1 tablespoon of the bean paste over the skin, top with 1 tablespoon sprouts, and top them with 1 tablespoon of the potato.

2. Mix the mashed tofu and shrimp together. Place 2 teaspoons of the mixture over the potato. Lastly, sprinkle 1/2 teaspoon crisp shallots over all.

3. Roll the flexible egg roll wrapper over to enclose the stuffing. Fold the ends in, first from the left, then from the right, and roll the cylinder over again to shape a roll about 3 1/2 inches long and 1 inch thick. Make spring rolls with the remaining ingredients in the same manner.

Serve these uncooked snacks at room temperature with tea or coffee.

MAKES 8 SPRING ROLLS.

SIDE DISHES, PICKLES, AND CONDIMENTS

Nothing inspires excitement when it comes to ethnic dining more than seeing the table covered with an assortment of side dishes. The Koreans are famous for this, and the Malaysians also enjoy seeing the table so replete with food that very little of the tablecloth is even visible.

Most of the side dishes, which include pickles and condiments, are vivid with *belacan*, ginger, or hot chili. This is predictable since the purpose of these dishes is to enliven the food and increase the appetite. An example that I find particularly pleasing and illustrative is Onion and Tamarind Side Dish (page 244), which is an Indian cre-

Setting up street food in Penang.

ation but compatible with the food of any Asian cuisine. Or, for that matter, American cooking.

Nothing ventured, nothing gained; make a selection of your favorites from the recipes that follow and include them frequently in your culinary repertoire.

KERABU TAUGE (ALL MALAYSIA)

Bean Sprout Side Dish

Although the Chinese invented bean sprouts and use them more than anyone else, sprouts have entered the mainstream and are included in dishes of both the Malays and Indians. Here is a good example of cross-culinary activity, and it is compatible with any kind of Malaysian food.

1/2 *pound fresh mackerel on the bone*
2 *cups water*
1 *teaspoon salt*
4 *shallots, sliced*
1 *teaspoon sliced ginger*
1/2 *teaspoon pepper*
1/2 *teaspoon sugar*
1 *teaspoon fresh lime juice*
1/2 *cup "thick" coconut milk (see page 14)*
1 *pound bean sprouts, blanched in hot water 3 minutes and drained well*

1. Cook the fish, covered, in the water with the salt over moderate heat for 15 minutes. Drain. Remove the meat from the bones, dice it, and discard the bones.
2. Process the shallots, ginger, pepper, sugar, lime juice, and coconut milk to a paste. Fold in the mackerel and bean sprouts.
    Serve at room temperature.

SERVES 6.

Kerabu Timun (Malay)

Cucumber and Fish Side Dish

An unusual combination in coconut milk sauce.

5   *young cucumbers*
1/2 *pound mackerel*
2   *shallots, sliced*
     a 1/2-inch piece ginger, sliced
1 1/4 *cups "regular" coconut milk (see page 14)*
1/2 *teaspoon salt, or to taste*
3/4 *teaspoon black pepper*
     lemon wedges for serving

1. Do not peel the cucumbers. Halve them lengthwise, remove the seeds, and slice into half moons.
2. Cook the mackerel in 2 cups water until soft, drain, let cool, and flake the meat. Discard the skin and bones. Set aside.
3. Process the shallots and ginger to a smooth paste with 1/4 cup of the coconut milk.
4. Now combine the paste with the balance of the coconut milk, salt, pepper, mackeral, and cucumbers. Toss like a salad.

Serve at room temperature with the lemon wedges as a side dish with seafood dishes.

SERVES 6.

KERABU TIMUN KACANG PANJANG (MALAY)

Cucumber and Longbean Side Dish

The *loobia,* or Chinese longbean, is like a western string bean that can grow twelve to fourteen inches in length on vines or low plants. I used them in India and Indonesia. They lend themselves to various Asian dishes and are compatible with almost any other vegetable. This *kerabu* is a good example of a side dish that goes well with any kind of Malaysian meat or seafood dishes.

1   *tablespoon vegetable oil*
4   *shallots, sliced thin*
1/3   *cup small fresh shrimp, peeled*
1   *medium onion, sliced into rings (1/2 cup)*
2   *young cucumbers, unpeeled but sliced*
1   *pound longbeans, trimmed and cut in 2-inch pieces*
1/2   *teaspoon salt*
1/2   *teaspoon sugar*
1/2   *cup green peas, fresh or frozen*

1.   Heat the oil in a wok or skillet, add the shallots, and stir-fry them over moderate heat until golden. Add the shrimp and stir-fry them for 1 minute.

2.   Now add the onion, cucumbers, longbeans, salt, and sugar and stir-fry for 3 minutes. Lastly, add the peas and stir-fry another minute. Adjust the salt and sugar to taste.

Serve warm as a side dish.

SERVES 8.

ACAR TIMUN NANAS (MALAY)

Cucumber and Pineapple Side Dish

Here is a fresh salad/chutney that's to be eaten during a meal with cooked dishes.

3   *young cucumbers, unpeeled, halved lengthwise, and cut into half moons*
1   *pound ripe fresh pineapple, peeled, cored, cut into 1-inch cubes*
2   *medium onions, sliced into rounds (1 cup)*
2   *fresh hot red chilis, seeded and sliced thin*
2   *fresh hot green chilis, seeded and sliced thin*
½   *teaspoon salt, or to taste*
½   *teaspoon sugar*
2   *tablespoons white vinegar*

Mix all the ingredients together. Adjust the sugar/vinegar for a mild sweet and sour flavor. Refrigerate.
   Serve cool.

SERVES 8.

KERABU TERONG PANJAN (MALAY)

Eggplant Side Dish

Side dishes are not meant to be the principal entrèe in a meal. They are an adjunct, no matter how tasty you might find them. This *kerabu* is a vegetarian preparation that is easy to assemble and easier to serve and goes with any kind of Malaysian meal or seafood dishes.

2	*tablespoons vegetable oil*
4	*shallots, sliced*
4	*cloves garlic, sliced*
	a 1/2-inch piece ginger, sliced thin
1/2	*teaspoon* belacan, *toasted (see Glossary)*
5	*Oriental eggplant (2 pounds), sliced on the diagonal 1/4 inch thick*
1/2	*teaspoon salt, or to taste*
1/4	*teaspoon sugar*

1. Heat the oil in a wok or skillet and stir-fry the shallots, garlic, ginger, and *belacan* over moderate heat until the shallots are golden, about 2 minutes.
2. Add the eggplant, salt, and sugar and continue to stir-fry until the eggplant has softened, about 3 minutes.

    Serve warm.

SERVES 8.

KERABU MANGGA (MALAY)

Green Mango and Anchovy Side Dish

2   *large julienne-sliced peeled green unripe mangoes (available at Hispanic and Asian markets)*

1   *carrot, peeled and julienne sliced (¹/₂ cup)*

¹/₂ cup ikan bilis, *crisp fried in oil (see Glossary)*

2   *shallots, sliced thin*

1   *teaspoon sugar*

¹/₄ *teaspoon salt*

3   *tablespoons crisp fried shallots (see How to Make, page 288)*

1   *tablespoon seeded and chopped fresh hot red chili*

2   *tablespoons fresh lime juice*

Mix all the ingredients together well. Toss the mixture to integrate the flavors.

Serve at room temperature as a side dish with any Malaysian food.

SERVES 6 TO 8.

KERABU MANGGA (MALAY)
Young Green Mango Side Dish

Many cultures use green unripe mango for salads or side dishes; I think immediately of Central America as well as tropical Asia. Unripe mango is tart, without being unpleasantly acidic and has a crunchy texture that lends itself to this Malaysian side dish.

½   *cup fresh grated coconut*
3   *fresh hot red chilis, sliced*
1   *teaspoon* belacan, *toasted (see Glossary)*
2   *tablespoons small dried shrimp (available at Asian markets)*
1   *stalk lemongrass, white part only, sliced*
1   *teaspoon sliced ginger*
½   *teaspoon salt, or to taste*
¼   *cup water*
2   *cups julienne-sliced, peeled green unripe mango (available at Hispanic and Asian markets)*

1.   Process everything but the mango with the water to a smooth paste. In a bowl mix the paste with the mango slices and toss well.

   Serve as a side dish with meat or fish dishes.

MAKES ABOUT 2½ CUPS, OR YOU MAY ALSO HALVE THE RECIPE.

NOTE Lemongrass may be a little hard to slice unless it is young and fresh. The bottom white part can be sliced by peeling away one or two of the outside layers to find the inner soft core. It can be sliced.

SAMBAL GORENG NENAS (MALAY)

Stir-Fried Pineapple Condiment

A fairytale told to me by a homecook in Kuantan: "Once upon a time the chili and tamarind were enemies. Now, when meeting together in the wok, they fight again, the hot chili against the sour tamarind. The chili is the trouble maker, agitator, and villain."

And I would add, with a little judicious juggling of the spices and seasonings, when the cooking is good all the ingredients are compatible.

1   *ripe fresh pineapple (about 3 pounds)*
4   *shallots, sliced*
3   *cloves garlic, sliced*
    a 1-inch piece ginger, sliced
1   *teaspoon* belacan, *toasted (see Glossary)*
3   *tablespoons water*
2   *tablespoons vegetable oil*
2   *tablespoons* chili boh, *or more, to taste (see How to Make, page 290)*
2   *tablespoons tamarind paste dissolved in* 1/4 *cup water, strained (see How to Make, page 289)*
1/2 *teaspoon salt*

1. Peel and core the pineapple. Cut it into quarters, then slice each quarter about 1/4 inch thick.
2. In a blender or food processor, process the shallots, garlic, ginger, *belacan,* and the water to a smooth paste.
3. Heat the oil in a wok or large skillet, add the shallot paste and *chili boh,* and stir-fry over low heat for 2 minutes.
4. Add the pineapple slices, tamarind liquid, and salt and stir-fry the mixture for 3 minutes. Cover and cook for 3 minutes more.

   Serve at room temperature with any Malay dish. The condiment may be refrigerated for 2 days.

   SERVES 10.

VARIATION To add variety to the condiment, add 1/2 cup small fresh shrimp, peeled and deveined, at the same time as the pineapple. Stir-fry for 3 minutes, cover, and cook for 3 minutes more.

Kerabu Ikan Bilis Kacang (Malay)

Crisp Baby Anchovies with Peanuts

A *kerabu*, or side dish, is to be served with others at a meal. In this traditional *kampong*-style side dish, the ever-popular baby anchovy is fried to a crisp and can be eaten out of hand, as is, or incorporated into a tempting stir fry. I like them either way, with a glass of rice wine.

oil for pan frying
1/2   *cup* ikan bilis *(see Glossary)*
4   *shallots, sliced*
4   *cloves garlic, sliced*
      a 1/2-inch piece ginger, sliced
1/2   *teaspoon* belacan, *toasted (see Glossary)*
1   *medium onion, sliced into rings (1/2 cup)*
1/2   *teaspoon sugar*
1/4   *teaspoon salt*
1/2   *cup roasted peanuts*

1.   Heat the oil in a skillet, add the *ikan bilis,* and stir-fry over low heat until light brown and crisp. (Since the fish are tiny this may take less than 1/2 minute.) Drain on paper towel.
2.   Process the shallots, garlic, ginger, and *belacan* to a paste.
3.   Reheat the oil in the skillet and stir-fry the garlic paste until it changes color, about 1 minute.
4.   Add the onion, sugar, and salt and stir-fry until combined. Add the crisp anchovies and peanuts, mix well, and stir-fry for 1 minute more.

      Serve warm or at room temperature.

SERVES 8.

Sambal Belacan (All Malaysia)

Fermented Shrimp Paste Condiment

Belacan is that traditional Malaysian shrimp paste that is sold in blocks and used in curries to give them more dimension without turning them "fishy." Note that *belacan* should be toasted lightly in the oven or in a toaster oven about 3 minutes. After that it is ready to be used.

Malaysians like a bite in their foods and this sambal answers that wish.

1   *tablespoon* belacan, *toasted (see Glossary)*
3   *or 4 fresh hot red chilis, seeded and sliced thin*
2   *tablespoons fresh lime juice*

> Blend the 3 ingredients in a food processor or with a mortar and pestle to a paste. (Malaysian kitchens often have as part of the equipment a stone grinder that is indispensable for daily use.)
>
> Serve as a dip with Chop Chai #1 (page 137) or any other preparation of choice.
>
> MAKES ¼ CUP.

CASSAVA (TAPIOCA) AND SWEET POTATOES

Cassava is grown in the hilly tropical countryside of Sabah and its characteristic spindly shape is easy to spot. Both the root and young leaves are eaten; the root is boiled plain and served with Sambal Belacan (above). The leaves are very tasty, and I have eaten them numerous times cooked in coconut milk with various seasonings.

There are three kinds of sweet potatoes—white, brown, and purple. The young leaves are also eaten as a form of spinach. The potatoes, like the cassava root, are boiled plain.

IKAN BILIS SAMBAL (MALAY INDIAN)

Dried Anchovy Side Dish

Remarkable baby anchovies here are first fried crisp in a small amount of oil, then combined with a garlicky, hot sauce. The anchovies are wonderful and also available, in Asian food markets in metropoli like New York City.

6   *tablespoons corn oil*
1   *cup* ikan bilis *(see Glossary)*
4   *cloves garlic, smashed with the flat side of a cleaver*
5   *shallots, sliced and lightly smashed*
3   *tablespoons hot red dried chili, toasted in a skillet, then crushed*
1/4 *teaspoon salt*

1.   Heat 4 tablespoons of the oil in a wok or skillet and stir-fry the *ikan bilis* over low heat for a minute or two to crisp them. Remove and set aside.
2.   Remove the oil. Add the remaining 2 tablespoons of oil to the wok and stir-fry the garlic over low heat for 1 minute. Add the shallots and stir-fry until they change color.
3.   Now add the crushed chili, crisp baby anchovies, and salt and toss well for 1 minute.
     Serve as a side dish at room temperature.

SERVES 6 OR MORE.

CHILI-HOT SIDE DISH (CHINESE)

This is a family recipe for a condiment from a friend in Ipoh.

1   *fresh hot red chili, sliced thin*
    a 1-inch piece ginger, sliced thin
½   *cup light soy sauce*
3   *cloves garlic, chopped fine*
2   *teaspoons fresh lime juice*

Mix everything together briskly.

Serve as a side dish or condiment with meat and seafood dishes.

Serve at room temperature.

MAKES ABOUT ½ CUP.

CHILI ACAR (CHINESE)
Pickled Chilis

Fresh green chilis are pickled here in a simple, straightforward manner. They are tasty and piquant, a good accompaniment to Asian meals and a frequent sight on Chinese tables in Malaysia.

1/2 *pound fresh green chilis, seeded and sliced thin*
1   *teaspoon salt*
1   *tablespoon sugar*
1   *cup white vinegar*

Mix everything together, and adjust the sweet and sour contrast by adding more sugar if wanted. Do not overdo this.

Store in a glass jar with a tight lid and let stand at room temperature 1 day before using. Refrigerate at all times.

MAKES 1 QUART.

PICKLED GINGER (CHINESE)

4 to 5 ounces young ginger, thinly sliced
2 tablespoons white vinegar
1 teaspoon sugar

Mix all the ingredients together and marinate, covered, 1 day in the refrigerator before using.

Serve with Asam Udang (page 147) as a side dish.

MAKES ABOUT ½ CUP.

VARIATION The same recipe can be made with young cucumbers: Use ½ pound (3 or 4), and do not peel. Slice the cucumbers thin and mix with the vinegar and sugar. Adjust the sweet and sour balance, if desired. Marinate as above, 1 day in the refrigerator before using.

TIMUN ACAR (INDIAN)

Cucumber Pickle

Pickles and side dishes are characteristic of Indian cooking. This recipe came from a wonderful banana-leaf restaurant where the rice, dal, curries—in fact, the entire meal—was served on a large banana leaf. Who needed plates!

  3   *tablespoons corn oil*
  2   *teaspoons black mustard seed*
  5   *cloves garlic, sliced*
  3   *medium onions, sliced (1 1/2 cups)*
2–3 *tablespoons hot red chili flakes, to taste*
  1   *pound carrots, sliced thin on the diagonal*
  2   *pounds young cucumbers (6), unpeeled but sliced thin*
  1   *teaspoon salt*
  2   *tablespoons white vinegar*

1. Heat the oil in a wok or large skillet over low heat, and add the mustard seed, which will pop when it hits the oil. Add the garlic, stir-fry a few moments, then add the onions and stir-fry until golden.

2. Add the chili flakes and continue to stir-fry until combined. Add the carrots, cucumbers, salt, and vinegar and toss for 5 minutes, combining the pickle well. Cool.

   The pickle may be eaten immediately but it is better to let it stand for 4 hours at room temperature before tasting. Covered, it can be stored in the refrigerator for 1 week.

MAKES MORE THAN A QUART, SERVING 8 OR MORE.

Acar Kuning (Indian)

Yellow Vegetable Pickle

Turmeric has a penetrating yellow color and that is what gives this pickle its name. This condiment is compatible with any Malay or Indian dishes.

2	tablespoons vegetable oil
1	teaspoon black mustard seed
4	shallots, quartered
	a 1½-inch piece ginger, julienne sliced
5	cloves garlic
½	teaspoon turmeric
1	pound young cucumbers (3), sliced little finger size, about 2 inches long
1	carrot, julienne sliced (¾ cup)
2	or 3 fresh hot chilis, seeded and julienne sliced
¼	cup white vinegar
1	tablespoon sugar
½	teaspoon salt
1	teaspoon toasted sesame seed

1. Heat the oil in a wok or large skillet and over low heat pop the mustard seed in the oil. Add all at once the shallots, ginger, garlic, and turmeric and stir-fry for 2 minutes.
2. Add the cucumbers, carrot, chilis, vinegar, sugar, and salt and continue to stir-fry for 3 minutes. Stir in the sesame seed. Cool to room temperature.

   May be stored, covered, in the refrigerator for 1 week.

SERVES 8 OR MORE.

Pudeena Chutney (Indian)

Mint Chutney

Here is a very fine side dish that is compatible with both Indian and Malay foods. It can be refrigerated for several days, but is best served at room temperature.

1   *cup fresh mint leaves*
    a 1-inch piece young ginger, sliced
1   *fresh hot red chili, seeded and sliced*
1   *shallot, sliced*
¼   *teaspoon salt*

Process all the ingredients together into a smooth paste in a food processor. (The consistency will be thick.)

MAKES ABOUT ⅔ CUP.

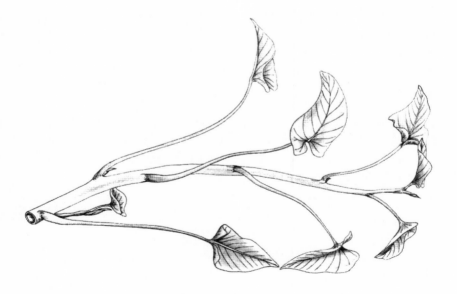

Sambal Tumis Bawang Besar (Indian Muslim)

Onion and Tamarind Side Dish

A chutney can be a very useful preparation in your culinary reper-toire. This one, with its wonderful tamarind flavor, hot chili, sugar, and crisp fried baby anchovies that are found in every Asian food shop, was prepared for me by an Indian Muslim family in Kuching, Sarawak, Borneo. That's a long distance to go for chutney but worth every mile.

3   *tablespoons vegetable oil*
1   *pound onions (4 medium), sliced (about 2 cups)*
1   *tablespoon crushed hot red dried chili*
½   *cup* ikan bilis *(see Glossary), fried crisp*
¼   *cup tamarind paste dissolved in 1 cup water, strained (see How to Make, page 289)*
1   *tablespoon sugar, or more, to taste*
½   *teaspoon salt*

1.   Heat the oil in a wok or pan, add the onions, and stir-fry over low heat until they turn golden. Add the chili and *ikan bilis* and stir-fry for 1 minute.
2.   Add the tamarind liquid and sugar and let the mixture simmer over low heat until much but not all of the liquid evaporates. (This may take about 5 minutes.) Let cool. The chutney can be refrigerated for 1 week.

Serve at room temperature as a side dish with Indian foods.

SERVES 8 OR MORE.

Sambal Belacan (Nonya)

Belacan Table Condiment

The Nonya prepare this simple side dish to liven up food that might need it. Rather than stir it into a meat or seafood dish, the diner adds it according to personal taste.

1   *teaspoon* belacan, *toasted (see Glossary)*
3   *fresh hot red chilis, sliced*
    juice of 1 lime (about 3 tablespoons)

> In a mortar and pestle pound the *belacan* with the chilis until thoroughly combined. Then stir in the lime juice.
>
> Serve in a bowl at the table. This sambal is best prepared fresh daily.
>
> MAKES ABOUT 3 TABLESPOONS.

Sambal Tauqua (Portuguese)

Salad of Cucumber and Tahu Side Dish

A well-seasoned salad cum side dish that the Malacca colonials have devised to tantalize their taste buds.

1 *large cucumber, peeled*
1 *square* tahu *(bean curd)*
   oil for deep frying
1 *or 2 fresh hot red chilis, to taste, sliced*
1 *clove garlic*
2 *tablespoons white vinegar*
2 *teaspoons sugar*
¼ *teaspoon salt*

1. Scrape the cucumber lengthwise with the tines of a fork to score it in a design. Cut it in half lengthwise, then slice each half into half moons.
2. In a skillet heat the oil, add the *tahu,* and brown it on all sides. Drain on paper towels. Cut into ¼-inch-thick little finger-sized slices.
3. Process the chilis, garlic, vinegar, sugar, and salt to a smooth paste.
4. Combine the paste with the cucumber and *tahu,* tossing gently.
   Serve as a side dish at room temperature.

SERVES 4.

BAMBANGAN (ETHNIC PEOPLE)
Wild Mango Pickle

It is unlikely that the large wild mango of Sabah is available in western regions, but I am including this recipe for historical purposes. As a substitute, use the small unripe green mangoes when they are available in season.

The seed of the mango plays an important part with the Kadazan tribe. Grated, then dried in the sun, it is sprinkled as a garnish on foods, such as Hinava (page 141). The freshly grated seed can also be used and the dried seed, too, during off season, when the mango is not available.

5   *unripe wild mangoes (use green unripe mangoes, available at Hispanic and Asian markets), peeled and sliced into 1-inch pieces*
1   *tablespoon salt*
1   *fresh hot red chili, cut into long julienne slices*

> Toss all the ingredients together and store in a glass container with a tight lid. Let the mixture stand in a warm place to mature for 2 days in the summer and 3 days in cooler weather.
>
> Serve with any kind of Kadazan food.

NOTE The mango seeds here can be grated, dried in the sun, and stored for off-season use.

SWEETS AND DESSERTS

The sweets and desserts of Malaysia are not your conventional continental conglomerations. They are idiosyncratic and unlike anything found in the West. How to explain attractive, tempting concoctions prepared from tapioca flour, sticky (glutinous) rice, pandan leaf juice, red, green, yellow, and sometimes blue coloring from a flower, or *gula Malacca*? Then there is rice flour, black rice, pearl sago, green mung beans, 100 egg yolks, mashed potatoes, grated cassava, and coconut milk in a dizzying array of combinations.

Most of the sweets are inventions of the Malay community but have filtered out to the the general public, who dote on them. Personally, I enjoy the taste and texture but also the kaleidoscopic appearance of a snack table covered with platters of these colorful sweets.

Market day in Malaysia.

BUBUR KACANG HIJAU (MALAY)

Green Bean Porridge

Malaysians like their porridges and there are several popular ones that are frequently served. These are not breakfast porridges, like oatmeal, but desserts prepared from unconventional ingredients. I like them very much after lunch or as a teatime, coffee-hour snack.

4 *cups water*
1 *cup green mung beans, rinsed*
¹/₄ *cup pearl sago soaked in water 10 minutes and drained*
1 *cup "regular" coconut milk (see page 14)*
¹/₄ *cup sugar*
2 *tablespoons* gula Malacca *(see Glossary) or brown sugar*
1 *teaspoon salt*

1. Bring the water to a boil, add the mung beans, and cook over moderate heat until the skins crack open, about ¹/₂ hour.
2. Add the drained pearl sago and cook for 15 minutes. Add the coconut milk, both sugars, and the salt. Bring to a boil and remove from the heat.

   Serve warm in small bowls.

SERVES 4 OR 5.

Sago Gula Melaka
(All Malaysia/Chinese)

Sago Pudding with Palm Sugar and Coconut Milk

The wild sago palm tree produces the starch that ultimately is transformed into pearl sago. Malaysia is one of the important producers and exporters of the pearls used in making desserts and sago flour.

Those beautiful transparent pearls are tasteless. The texture is what counts. Here sago is topped with a rich sugar palm syrup, then bathed in coconut milk. It is certainly my favorite Malaysian dessert.

The Sago

1   *cup pearl sago, soaked in water ¹/₂ hour and drained*
4   *cups water*

The Syrup

1   *cup* gula Malacca *(see Glossary)*
2   *cups water*
1   *cup "regular" coconut milk (see page 14)*

1. Prepare the sago: Bring the water to a boil, add the sago, and simmer it over low heat until transparent, about 5 minutes. Stir once or twice as it thickens.
2. Strain and rinse under cold water. Transfer the sago to individual bowls or to one large dessert bowl and let it set 1 hour.
3. Prepare the syrup: Cook the *gula Malacca* and water over low heat for 10 minutes to thicken into a syrup. Cool well. Store in a jar in the refrigerator.
4. To serve, unmold the sago simply by prying it out of the bowls or slicing it in generous chunks and serving it in small bowls.

Pour 2 tablespoons of the syrup over it and add 2 tablespoons of the coconut milk or more to taste over that.

Serve cold.

SERVES 8.

NOTE For those that like the flavor of pandan, an optional choice is to add a pandan leaf to the syrup as it simmers. Remove it before cooling and storing the syrup.

Pengat Labu Manis (Malay)

Sweet Pumpkin Porridge

The public markets in several Malaysian cities featured the hard-shelled Cuban pumpkin with its smooth outer skin. Cuban pumpkins have a sweet orange-colored flesh and I find them in Caribbean groceries in New York City. If they are unavailable to you, use butternut squash, which is satisfactory in a pinch.

2   *pounds Cuban pumpkin (see above)*
1/2 *cup pearl sago soaked in water 10 minutes and drained*
4   *cups "regular" coconut milk (see page 14)*
1/2 *cup water*
1/4 *teaspoon salt*
1/2 *cup sugar*

1.   Peel the pumpkin and cut it into 1-inch cubes. Cook in water until soft, about 20 minutes. Drain.
2.   Mix the drained pearl sago, coconut milk, water, and salt together in a pan. Bring to a boil over low heat, stir in the sugar, and simmer for 10 minutes. Add the cooked pumpkin cubes and simmer for 5 minutes. Remove from the heat.

Serve warm in bowls for high tea or at any other snack time.

SERVES 8.

Pulut Hitam (Malay)

Black Rice Porridge

The state of Kedah in northeast Malaysia is a beautiful rice-growing area. Driving through the countryside en route to Alor Setar, the capital, one can see nothing but green all the way to the horizon. Yet black rice is not grown in Kedah, but across the border in Thailand, a contradiction that was not explained to me.

I learned this very popular dish from a *mikchik,* an elderly lady known as Auntie.

The Porridge

8 *cups water*
1 *cup black rice (pulut), well rinsed, soaked in water overnight, and drained*
1 *pandan leaf (see Glossary) or a drop of pandan essence*
³/₄ *cup sugar*
¹/₂ *cup dried longan fruit (optional)*

The Sauce

1 *cup "regular" coconut milk (see page 14)*
¹/₂ *cup water*
¹/₄ *teaspoon salt*

1. Prepare the porridge: Bring the water to a boil in a large pan over moderate heat. Add the rice and pandan leaf and reduce the heat to low. Add the sugar and dried longan, if using. Cook for 15 minutes, or until the rice is soft.
2. Make the sauce: Mix together the coconut milk, water, and salt and set aside.

    To serve, put the rice porridge in bowls. Serve the coconut milk mixture in another bowl.

Each person takes a portion of the coconut milk and pours it over the porridge. Or, as is often done, the porridge and coconut milk are mixed together in the kitchen.

Serve hot or at room temperature.

SERVES 8.

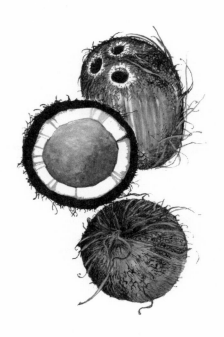

KUIH LAPIS (MALAY)
Red-and-White-Layered Custard

Another in the assortment of traditional custard sweets so beloved by the Malaysian public. This one is in red and white layers. One could add more layers depending upon the amount of custard mixture and number of servings desired.

2 *cups water*
1½ *cups sugar*
4 *cups "regular" coconut milk (see page 14)*
3 *cups flour*
1 *cup tapioca flour*
⅛ *teaspoon salt*
⅛ *teaspoon red food coloring*

1. Mix the water and sugar together in a pan. Bring to a boil to dissolve the sugar.
2. In a bowl mix together the coconut milk, flour, tapioca flour, and salt. Pour in the hot sugar syrup and mix together. Divide the mixture into 2 equal portions. Mix one part with the red coloring; the other portion remains white.
3. Prepare the layers: Take a Pyrex baking pan (8 or 9 inches square) in which the custard is to be steamed and preheat it by steaming it empty over hot water for 5 minutes. Pour in enough of the plain custard to form a layer ¼ inch thick. Steam it for 5 minutes to set. Now add a layer of the red custard ¼ inch thick and steam, covered, over hot water for 5 minutes. Repeat this sequence 2 more times. Now you have a 6-layered firm custard. Cool well.

   To serve, cut into 2-inch diamond shapes.

   SERVES 10.

SERI MUKA (MALAY)

Green-and-White Rice Custard

Malaysian sweets are often tinted with food coloring, such as green, and red and the odd blue. This one is two-tone, and is not only attractive to look at but smooth-textured as well.

This is a large recipe, enough for a good-sized party. I suggest that you prepare one half the recipe the first time you make it to inspire you to attempt more of these traditional sweets.

3	cups "regular" coconut milk (see page 14)
2	cups water
2	cups glutinous rice soaked in water overnight and drained
1	egg, beaten
1	cup sugar
2	teaspoons pandan leaf juice (see Note)
1/4	teaspoon green food coloring
1	cup flour
1/8	teaspoon salt

1. Mix 1 cup of the coconut milk and 1 cup of the water together. Add to the glutinous rice in a bowl. Steam the rice, covered, over hot water for 15 to 20 minutes until cooked. Press the rice firmly into a metal or glass tray. Set aside.
2. In a bowl mix the remaining 2 cups coconut milk and 1 cup water together with the egg, sugar, pandan juice, and food coloring. Add the flour and salt and combine well. Strain the mixture through a metal sieve to eliminate any lumps.
3. Pour the coconut milk mixture over the packed rice in the tray. Steam the tray, covered, over hot water until the custard becomes firm, about 20 minutes. Remove from the steamer and cool well.

    To serve, cut in the traditional diamond shape.

SERVES 10.

NOTE How to make pandan leaf juice: Combine $^1/_4$ cup of thinly sliced fresh or frozen pandan leaf with $^1/_4$ cup water and process until finely chopped. Strain the green juice through a metal sieve into a jar. Use what is required and refrigerate the balance, covered, for future use.

BUBUR SOM SOM (MALAY)
Traditional Malay Creme Caramel

A celebration of one sort or another is an opportunity for the homemaker to prepare the traditional Malay creme caramel. It is rich with coconut milk and sweetened with their remarkable dark palm sugar. I suggest halving this recipe as a more practical approach to making this tasty dessert.

10   *cups "regular" coconut milk (see page 14)*
 2   *cups rice flour*
½   *teaspoon salt*
 1   *cup* gula Malacca *(see Glossary)*
 3   *cups water*

1. Put the coconut milk, rice flour, and salt in a large pan and stir frequently over low heat for ½ hour. (The mixture will come to a boil and thicken.)
2. Pour the custard into a large flat tray with sides about 1 inch high or into mixing bowls. Refrigerate.
3. In a saucepan dissolve the *gula Malacca* in the water and bring to a boil over low heat. Simmer for 15 minutes, then strain through a metal sieve into a bowl. Let cool.

   To serve, scoop out portions of the custard into small cups or bowls and pour the syrup generously over the top.

   Serve cool.

SERVES 20.

ONDE ONDE (MALAY)

Sweet Rice Flour Balls

These delectable little rice balls are stuffed with *gula Malacca*, dark palm sugar, boiled, then rolled in shredded coconut. As simple as that and they are found all over Malaysia.

1 *pound glutinous rice flour*
¼ *teaspoon salt*
½ *cup water*
½ *cup* gula Malacca *(see Glossary)*
1 *cup shredded unsweetened coconut*

1. Mix the rice flour, salt, and water together to form a manageable dough. Shape the dough, 1 heaping teaspoonful at a time, into a small ball. Push a hole in the ball with your finger. Fill with about ¼ teaspoon of the *gula Malacca* and close over the hole. Fill all the dough balls in the same manner.
2. Bring a large pan of water to a boil over moderate heat. Add the balls, one by one, and cook for 2 to 3 minutes. When the balls float to the surface they are cooked and the sugar will have melted inside them. Remove with a slotted spoon and roll in the shredded coconut.

    Serve at room temperature, as a snack or dessert.

MAKES ABOUT 30 BALLS.

LOMPANG (MALAY)

Steamed Palm Sugar and Coconut Cakes

As with so many Malaysian sweets, only a few telling ingredients are necessary. More often than not, little cupcakes or diamond-shaped layered sweets are made with rice flour, as this one from Ipoh is.

$^1/_3$ *cup* gula Malacca *(see Glossary)*
1   *cup water*
$^2/_3$ *cup rice flour mixed with* $^1/_4$ *cup water*
$^1/_4$ *cup unsweetened dessicated coconut mixed with* $^1/_8$ *teaspoon salt*

1. Mix all the ingredients together to a smooth consistency.
2. Heat individual porcelain cups with a capacity of at least 3 tablespoons in a steamer. (Small Chinese rice wine cups will do fine.) Pour in not more than 3 tablespoons of the coconut mixture. Steam, covered, over hot water for 15 to 20 minutes. To test for doneness, push a toothpick into the cakes. If it comes out dry, they are ready.

    Serve in the cups at room temperature, with tea or coffee. Or unmold, if desired.

MAKES ABOUT 20 CUPCAKES.

BINGKA KENTANG (ALL MALAYSIA)

Potato Cake

Not really a cake, these are usually served as sweet tidbits in one-inch squares, with the potato and coconut milk providing the smooth, melting texture and flavor. They are best eaten at room temperature during the coffee or tea hour.

1   *tablespoon margarine for greasing the 8-inch pan*
2   *cups mashed potatoes (about ¹/₂ pound)*
2   *cups "regular" coconut milk (see page 14)*
³/₄ *cup sugar*
1   *cup flour*
3   *eggs, beaten*
¹/₂ *teaspoon salt*
1   *or 2 drops yellow food coloring*

1.   Grease a Pyrex or metal 8-inch square baking pan and preheat the oven to 350 -degrees.
2.   Process all the ingredients together by hand or in a food processor until smooth.
3.   Pour the mixture into the prepared pan and bake for 35 or 40 minutes, or until the top is light brown in color. Let the cake cool and cut into 1-inch squares. Can be stored in the refrigerator for 2 days.

SERVES 10 TO 12.

Kueh Bakar
(also called Bingka Tepung) (Malay)

Green Cake

This cake, which is green due to the coloring of pandan leaf juice, is richly endowed with thick coconut milk. It is a very traditional Malay sweet that is also a basic recipe that can be modified. In the state of Negeri Sembilan, an assortment of spices are added to enrich the flavor. Canned creamed corn, an American invention, has also been known to have been included in the batter on occasion.

During the British colonial era and in small villages it was rare to find a modern oven. To bake the cake, a solid pottery or metal dish was filled with the batter and placed on a charcoal fire. The cover of the dish was piled with hot charcoal embers that were intended to duplicate the all-enveloping heat of an oven.

1	*tablespoon butter or margarine, softened, for greasing the pan*
4	*eggs*
1	*cup sugar*
1/8	*teaspoon salt*
1³/4	*cups flour*
3	*cups "thick" coconut milk (see page 14)*
³/4	*cup water*
2	*tablespoons pandan juice (see Note, page 257)*
1	*drop green food coloring*
2	*tablespoons sesame seeds, toasted*

1. Rub an 8-inch square baking pan with the butter or margarine. Preheat the oven to 350 -degrees.
2. Beat the eggs until foamy, add the sugar and salt, and mix well. Stir in the flour until blended.
3. Add the coconut milk, water, and pandan juice plus a drop of green food coloring.

4. Pour the batter into the prepared pan, sprinkle the sesame seeds over it, and bake for 40 to 45 minutes. The cake should be soft and melting. Cool.

To serve, slice into 2-inch squares.

SERVES 10 TO 12.

Ketayap (Malay)
Stuffed Coconut Pancakes

These tasty pancakes are green. One sees them for sale in public markets where the ladies sell their sweets. Green coloring for food is sold in small bottles and used sparingly. As far as I was able to ascertain, there is no symbolic reason for the color green in these, but Malaysians like it.

The Pancakes

²/₃ cup flour
1   egg, beaten
1   cup water
¹/₈ teaspoon salt
1   or 2 drops green food coloring
    oil for the skillet

The Stuffing

1   cup grated coconut, unsweetened dessicated or freshly grated
¹/₃ cup sugar
1   tablespoon water
¹/₄ teaspoon vanilla
1   tablespoon flour

1. Prepare the pancakes: Mix all the ingredients together, except the oil, into a smooth batter. Pour through a metal sieve into a bowl to remove any lumps.
2. Rub the skillet, preferably nonstick, with oil. Pour in 2 tablespoons of the batter, spread it over the skillet, to make a thin pancake about 5 to 6 inches in diameter, and fry 1 minute only over low heat. Remove and set aside. Make pancakes with the remaining batter in the same manner.

3. Prepare the stuffing: In a bowl mix the coconut, sugar, water, and vanilla together. In a skillet without oil stir-fry it over low heat for 3 minutes. Stir in the flour and stir-fry for 2 minutes more. Remove from the heat.

4. Stuff each pancake: Place 2 tablespoons of the stuffing near the edge of the lower half of the pancake. Fold over once, then fold the right side and left side to the middle and over once more to make a cylinder 3½ inches long and 1 inch thick. Transfer to a platter.

    Serve the pancakes at room temperature as a snack with tea or coffee.

MAKES 15 STUFFED PANCAKES.

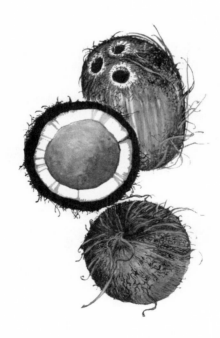

Rebus Pisang Sabah (All Sabah)

Boiled Honey Bananas with Coconut

Honey bananas are about 3½ inches long and quite common in Asian markets. They are the "local" food of Sabah; that is to say, a common everyday type of sweet.

6 *ripe honey bananas*
¼ *cup sugar*
½ *cup confectioner's sugar*
1 *cup grated fresh coconut*

1. Cook the bananas in boiling water in their skins until soft, about 10 minutes. Peel and put them on a serving platter.
2. Mix together both of the sugars and the grated coconut. Roll the bananas in this mixture and arrange in a single layer back on the platter.

     Serve at room temperature as a snack during tea or coffee time.

SERVES 6.

PENGAT PISANG (MALAY)

Banana Sweets for Ramadan

A friend in Sabah described this dessert to me, which was served in the evening when his family broke the fast of Ramadan.

  2   *cups "regular" coconut milk (see page 14)*
 1/2 *cup* gula Malacca *(see Glossary) or brown sugar*
 1/4 *teaspoon salt*
  1   *tablespoon pearl sago soaked in water 1/2 hour and drained*
  8   *small ripe honey bananas, peeled and cut into 1-inch pieces*

1. Put the coconut milk, *gula Malacca*, salt, pearl sago in a pan and bring to a boil over low heat. Mix well and simmer 10 minutes, stirring occasionally.
2. Add the bananas and simmer for 10 minutes more.
   Serve warm or at room temperature in dessert bowls.

SERVES 8.

Akak (Malay)
Royal Cupcakes

I was privileged to be invited into the home kitchen of Hajjah Nik Faizah, the royal cook of the Sultan of Kelantan in Kota Bahru, to see how the royal sweets are made. The kitchen, of ample size, was in a shed outside the home and was a combination of eighteenth-century techniques and modern times, with a mobile phone on the kitchen table at the ready for any culinary emergency.

The old-time kitchen stove for cakes consisted of a substantial fire of dried coconut husks fitted into a metal brazier that in turn fitted over the top of the cupcake tin. The square cupcake tins for this recipe are made of solid iron with thirty-six round concave depressions for the cakes. Heat was produced on the top of the tins by the burning husks mixed with charcoal. The bottom part of this simulated oven was a similar fire, with the cupcake tin in the middle.

Nowadays the oven has been modified so that the heat on the bottom has been replaced by a gas burner on the floor of the kitchen, a modern touch, while the top heat is still provided by the coconut-husk fire in the brazier. The intense heat from the top and bottom baked the cakes in 3 minutes.

1	*cup* gula Malacca *(see Glossary)*
1/4	*cup water*
2	*cups "regular" coconut milk (see page 14)*
1	*pandan leaf or 1/8 teaspoon essence (see Glossary)*
1/2	*cup flour*
10	*eggs, beaten*

1. Preheat the oven to 350 degrees. Lightly oil cupcake tins.
2. Dissolve the *gula Malacca* in the water and bring to a boil over low heat. Add the coconut milk and pandan leaf or essence. Turn off the heat and mix in the flour until smooth and thorough combined. Stir in the eggs, beating until combined.

3. Fill the cupcake tins with batter. Bake for 15 minutes, or until a wooden skewer, inserted in the cakes, comes out clean. Cool.

MAKES 30 CAKES.

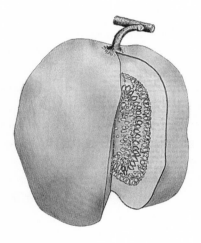

Jala Mas (Malay)
Golden Nets

This recipe, frankly, is submitted for historical purposes rather than as a sweet I want you to reproduce in your home. It is the most unusual, if not the strangest, recipe I have ever encountered. I watched this being made at the Sultan's palace with the techniques of yesteryear. A jala is a fisherman's net (see page 217 for further explanation).

6 *pounds sugar*
8 *cups water*
100 *egg yolks strained through a metal strainer, but not beaten*
cold water

1. Mix the sugar and water together in a very large pan and bring to a boil over low heat. Simmer the sugar syrup slowly.
2. (In olden times a 5-inch cone was made by twisting a banana leaf into a funnel shape, leaving a hole in the bottom ⅛ inch in diameter. Now the cone is made of stainless steel, with a hole in the bottom to pour the egg yolks into the hot syrup.) Now pour ¼ cup of the yolks into the cone held over the simmering syrup. Turn the cone rapidly clockwise until it empties. Thin orange strands of cooked yolk will form. Then pour ¼ cup cold water into the syrup, which stops the cooking process. Then with a very long chopstick lift the thin strands of cooked yolk out, and fold them back and forth into a bundle on a tray. Prepare the bundles this way until all the egg yolks are used.

   The bundles are eaten at room temperature.

MAKES 50 BUNDLES.

PUTIH TELUR
Egg White Jam

In the royal Jala Mas (previous recipe), 100 egg yolks are used in an extravagant display. It was logical that a culinary invention would take care of the remaining 100 whites. As a result, we have this sweet white jam, which is eaten with bread.

When I saw this being made, one of the *mikchiks* ("aunties") helping in the kitchen was crouched on the floor stirring a very large pan over a single gas burner. The almost-continuous stirring over low heat develops the whites into a thick, smooth white texture and with time into royal jam.

3	*pounds sugar*
1/2	*cup flour*
100	*egg whites strained through a metal sieve*
3/4	*cup vegetable oil*
1	*fresh pandan leaf or 1 drop pandan essence (see Glossary)*

1. In a very large bowl mix the sugar and flour together. Add the egg whites and oil and mix well. Transfer to a large pan.
2. Cook the mixture over low heat, stirring continuously. After 1/2 hour, when half cooked, add the pandan leaf or essence. Continue cooking another 1/2 hour, until the mixture is thick and smooth—a jam.

    Serve at room temperature with bread at teatime.

    SERVES 50.

NOTE A *mikchik* is an old "auntie" who makes unusual sweets in quantities for restaurants and catering activities. One does not have to prepare sweets with 100 eggs when the *mikchik* can make a few dozen for teatime.

Buah Tanjung (Malay)

Tear Drops

I offer this recipe for historical purposes. *Tanjung* in the Malay title for the recipe is a local fruit of Kelantan state, which is where I saw these unique sweets being prepared by the Sultan's cook.

The royal cooks are a hereditary group passing on their skill and knowledge to a female member of the family. Hajjah, the Sultan's cook, inherited her position from her mother, who inherited it from *her* mother. It was expected. Now, Hajjah's fifteen-year-old daughter is learning the trade so that she can take over as cook upon her mother's retirement. Getting back to the title of this wonderful treat, the fruit looks like a tear drop as it falls. The buah is the same shape, but yellow as the egg yolks.

10	*egg yolks*
⅓	*cup rice flour*
1	*pound sugar*
1⅓	*cups water*

1. Mix the yolks and rice flour together slowly but thoroughly, with a spoon not a processor.
2. Prepare a sugar syrup as directed on page 270, but make it twice: once simmering *hot* (as in Jala Mas) and once again, prepared and then *cooled*.
3. With 3 fingers, remove ½ teaspoon of the batter and drop it into the simmering hot syrup. When the batter floats, after about 2 minutes, remove with a slotted spoon and put in the cooled syrup for 3 minutes. Remove. The tear drops are ready.

    Serve at room temperature with tea or coffee.

MAKES ABOUT 50 TEAR DROPS.

MALAY WEDDING MENU FROM KUANTAN

A Malay friend in the city of Kuantan on the east coast of Malaysia gave me the menu and recipes for his recent ceremonial wedding. These are all popular dishes that also could be used for other joyous occasions.

NASI MINYAK
Wedding Rice
or
NASI BUKAHARI
Wedding Rice with Meat

AYAM MASAK MERAH
Red-Cooked Chicken

DAGING RENDANG ROK
Grandfather's Beef Rendang

DALCA SAYUR
Malay Vegetable Curry

PACERI NENAS
Pineapple Side Dish

ACER JELATAH
Wedding Vegetable Pickle

Chinese dragon mural, Kuching, Sarawak.

Nasi Minyak

Wedding Rice

2   *tablespoons* ghee *(clarified butter, see Note below) or oil*
4   *shallots, sliced*
3   *cloves garlic, sliced*
     a 1-inch piece ginger, cut into julienne strips
2   *pandan leaves or* ¹/₈ *teaspoon pandan essence (optional, see Glossary)*
     a 1-inch piece cinnamon stick
2   *whole star anise*
2   *whole cloves*
3   *whole cardamom pods*
¹/₂   *cup evaporated or fresh milk*
2   *cups water*
2   *cups long-grain rice*
1   *teaspoon salt, or to taste*
2   *scallions, sliced, for garnish*
¹/₄   *cup raisins for garnish*
¹/₄   *cup cashews, roasted, for garnish*

1.   Heat the *ghee* or oil in a skillet, add the shallots, garlic, ginger, and pandan if using, and stir-fry over low heat for 2 minutes.
2.   Add the cinnamon stick, star anise, cloves, cardamom (called *rempah*, but also known as the "four brothers") and stir-fry for 2 minutes.
3.   Now add the milk and water and bring to a boil over moderate heat. Add the rice and reduce the heat to low. Cover the pan and simmer over very low heat for 20 to 25 minutes.

    Garnish with the scallions, raisins, and cashew nuts.

SERVES 8.

NOTE *Ghee*, the paramount Indian butter-oil, is preferred since it provides to those who are accustomed to it a pleasant and desirable aroma.

NASI BUKAHARI (MALAY)

Wedding Rice with Meat

This highly ornate rice is reserved for weddings and other important celebrations. Traditional Malay spices and seasonings, along with diced meat, enhance the flavors, and the dish is well garnished with raisins and nuts. There is something of India and the Middle East in all of this.

3	*tablespoons vegetable oil*
4	*shallots, sliced*
	a 1-inch piece young ginger, sliced
3	*cloves garlic, sliced*
1	*pandan leaf (optional, see Glossary)*
5	*curry leaves*
3	*whole dried hot red chilis*
1/4	*teaspoon curry powder*
1/4	*teaspoon ground fennel*
1/4	*teaspoon ground cumin*
1/4	*teaspoon ground coriander*
2	*cups fresh milk*
1	*teaspoon salt, or to taste*
3/4	*cup diced cooked beef, lamb, or chicken*
1/2	*cup water*
4	*cups long-grain rice, well rinsed*
3	*tablespoons raisins for garnish*
3	*tablespoons roasted cashews for garnish*
3	*tablespoons chopped fresh coriander for garnish*

1. Put the oil in a large pan, add the shallots, ginger, garlic, pandan leaf if using, curry leaves, and chilis, and stir-fry over low heat for 2 minutes.

2. Add the curry powder and ground fennel, cumin, and coriander and stir well. Add the milk, salt, meat, water, and rice, mix, and

bring to a boil. Cover the pan and simmer over low heat for 15 to 20 minutes. Stir once or twice and if too dry add several tablespoons water.

Serve warm garnished with the raisins, cashew nuts, and coriander.

SERVES 8 TO 10, WITH OTHER DISHES.

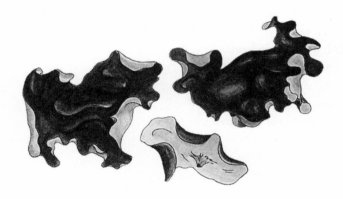

Ayam Masak Merah (Malay)

Red-Cooked Chicken

3   pounds chicken parts (12 pieces)
2   teaspoons salt
1   cup vegetable oil for deep frying
4   shallots, sliced
3   cloves garlic, sliced
    a 1½-inch piece ginger, sliced
2   tablespoons water
    a 2-inch piece cinnamon stick
3   whole cloves
3   whole star anise
4   cardamom pods
2   tablespoons chili boh (see How to Make, page 290)
1   tablespoon tamarind paste dissolved in 3 tablespoons water, strained (see How to Make, page 289)
½   cup evaporated milk
½   cup "thick" coconut milk (see page 14)
1   teaspoon sugar
2   scallions, sliced, for garnish
1   small onion, sliced into rings, for garnish

1.   Rub the chicken with the salt and let stand ½ hour.
2.   Heat the oil in a wok or large skillet and fry the chicken over low heat, turning it, for 5 minutes. Set aside on paper towels to drain. Remove all but 2 tablespoons of the oil.
3.   Process the shallots, garlic, and ginger with the water to a smooth paste.

4. Heat the 2 tablespoons oil in the wok or skillet and add the cinnamon stick, cloves, star anise, and cardamom pods and stir-fry over low heat for 1 minute. Add the shallot paste and *chili boh* and continue to stir-fry until combined well.
5. Stir in the tamarind liquid, then the milk, and simmer for 2 minutes. Add the chicken and fry it, basting occasionally, for 20 minutes.
6. Add the coconut milk and sugar and bring the mixture to a boil, stirring to dissolve the sugar, which completes the cooking.
    Serve warm garnished with the scallions and onion rings.

SERVES 8.

DAGING RENDANG TOK (MALAY)

Grandfather's Beef Rendang

This *rendang* is the groom's grandfather's favorite and was served at my friend's wedding.

3	tablespoons chili boh (see How to Make, page 290)
3	shallots, sliced
4	cloves garlic, sliced
	a 1½-inch piece ginger, sliced
	a 1-inch piece galangal (see Glossary), sliced
3	cups "light" coconut milk (see page 14)
1½	pounds lean boneless beef chuck, cut into 1-inch cubes
1	tablespoon tamarind paste dissolved in ¼ cup water, strained (see How to Make, page 289)
2	stalks lemongrass, bottom 5 inches, cracked
2	turmeric leaves (optional)
2	tablespoons brown sugar
½	teaspoon salt, or to taste
1	cup "thick" coconut milk (see page 14)
2	tablespoons grated unsweetened dessicated coconut

1. Process the *chili boh*, shallots, garlic, ginger, and galangal with ½ cup of the light coconut milk to a smooth paste. Marinate the beef, covered, in the paste in the refrigerator overnight.

2. The next day, bring the balance of the light coconut milk to a boil over low heat. Add the tamarind liquid, the lemongrass, and turmeric leaves if using, the beef, and its marinade. As it simmers, stir it slowly now and then. Add the brown sugar and salt. As the liquid evaporates, add the thick coconut milk and continue stirring until combined.

3. Toast the grated coconut in a nonstick skillet until brown. (This is known as *kerisek*.) Then crush it in a mortar and pestle or in

a processor and add it to the curry. Simmer over low heat, about 1 hour, or more, until all the liquid has evaporated. The beef will be moist and tender, but will be without sauce.

SERVES 8.

DALCA SAYUR (MALAY)

Malay Vegetable Curry

A Malay wedding is a time for a celebration, and this curry is luxuriously seasoned with aromatic spices and enriched with coconut milk. A heavy hand provides an enticing production.

5	*shallots, sliced*
3	*cloves garlic, sliced*
	a 1-inch piece ginger, sliced
2	*tablespoons water*
2	*tablespoons vegetable oil*
	a 1-inch piece cinnamon stick
3	*whole star anise*
3	*whole cloves*
3	*cardamom pods*
1/2	*teaspoon turmeric*
1	*teaspoon curry powder*
2	*cups "regular" coconut milk (see page 14)*
2	*small potatoes, cut into 1-inch cubes (1 1/2 cups)*
1	*carrot, cut into 1/2-inch dice (1 cup)*
1	*eggplant (1/2 pound), cut into 2-inch wedges*
5	*longbeans (loobia), cut into 2-inch pieces*
1	*medium onion, quartered*
1/2	*cup cooked yellow split peas*
1/4	*cup tamarind paste dissolved in 1/2 cup water, strained (see How to Make, page 289)*
1/2	*teaspoon salt*
2	*small ripe tomatoes, cut into 8 wedges*

1. Process the shallots, garlic, and ginger with the water to a paste.
2. Heat the oil in a wok or skillet, add the shallot paste, and stir-fry it over low heat for 2 minutes. Add the cinnamon stick, star anise, cloves, and cardamom pods and stir-fry another minute.

Stir in the turmeric and curry powder and combine well, stirring.

3. Add the coconut milk and bring to a boil over low heat. Add the potatoes and carrot and cook until soft, about 10 minutes. Then add the eggplant, beans, onion, and split peas. Simmer for 5 minutes. Add the tamarind liquid and salt and simmer 5 minutes more. Lastly, fold in the tomato wedges.

Serve warm as a side dish.

SERVES 8.

Paceri Nenas (Malay)

Pineapple Side Dish

1   ripe pineapple (about 2 to 3 pounds)
3   shallots, sliced
3   cloves garlic, sliced
    a 1-inch piece ginger, sliced
2   tablespoons plus 1 cup water
2   tablespoons corn oil
    a 1-inch piece cinnamon stick
3   whole star anise
3   whole cloves
4   cardamom pods
1/2 teaspoon turmeric
1   teaspoon curry powder
1/2 cup "regular" coconut milk (see page 14)
1/2 teaspoon salt, or to taste
2   tablespoons sugar

1. Peel and core the pineapple and cut it into quarters lengthwise. Slice each quarter in 1/4-inch-thick slices. Set aside.
2. Process the shallots, garlic, and ginger with the 2 tablespoons water to a smooth paste.
3. Heat the oil in a skillet, add the shallot paste, and stir-fry it over low heat 2 minutes. Add the cinnamon stick, star anise, cloves, and cardamom pods and stir-fry another minute.
4. Add the turmeric, curry powder, and 1 cup water and bring to a boil. Add the pineapple and simmer, covered, for 15 minutes. Add the coconut milk, salt, and sugar, mix well, and simmer for 2 minutes.

    Serve at room temperature.

SERVES 8 TO 10.

ACAR JELATAH (MALAY)

Wedding Vegetable Pickle

½ pineapple, peeled, cored, halved, and sliced thin
1 young cucumber, unpeeled and sliced very thin
2 fresh hot red chilis, seeded and sliced into julienne strips
2 medium onions, sliced into thin rounds (1 cup)
½ teaspoon salt
2 tablespoons sugar
3 tablespoons white vinegar

Combine all ingredients well and let stand for 1 hour before serving.

Serve at room temperature.

SERVES 8.

HOW TO MAKE BASICS

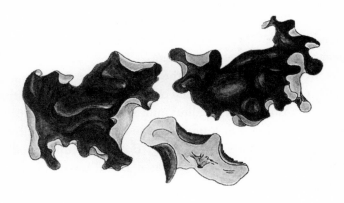

HOW TO MAKE FRESH COCONUT MILK

Fresh coconut milk can be made at home. There was a time when I prepared fresh coconut milk for all my Indonesian and other Southeast Asian recipes. When homemade in quantity, it can be frozen in plastic containers, thereby insuring an easy and accessible source.

1 *ripe coconut with a brown husk*
hot water

1. Bake the whole coconut in a preheated 350-degree oven for 15 minutes. The brown husk may crack during this time, which is an advantage. (The coconut pulp inside will be loosened by the heat and be much easier to remove.)

2. Remove the coconut from the oven and put it in a paper bag. With a hammer crack it open over the sink. The liquid that runs out is the water. The coconut milk is locked in the pulp. Pry the pulp out with a dull knife to prevent cutting yourself. Cut the pulp into thin slices ½ inch long. Prepare 2 cups sliced pulp in a blender with 2½ cups hot water. Blend for ½ minute, which will reduce the pulp to fragments and produce the coconut

milk. Repeat by 2-cup measures until all the pulp is utilized. (You should have about 5 cups milk or more.)

3. Pour the milk through a metal sieve into a bowl and squeeze out the pulp, a handful at a time. Discard the pulp or reserve it for another purpose.

What you now have is a standard strength coconut milk, which can be used for any recipe in this book without further dilution.

Let the milk settle in the bowl for 15 minutes before pouring into individual containers. Fragments of husk will settle to the bottom and can be discarded.

How to Make Crisp Fried Shallots

1   cup *shallots*
1   cup corn oil for *deep frying*

1.   Peel and slice the shallots into thin rounds. Separate the layers to insure uniform crispness.
2.   Heat the oil in a wok or skillet. Add the shallots and fry over low heat for about 5 minutes; cook them slowly, stirring frequently, so that they do not burn.
3.   When the shallots turn tan in color, remove them quickly with a slotted spoon and drain on paper towels to remove the excess oil. The shallots become crisp at this stage. Cool well and store in a glass jar with a tight cover. Refrigeration is not necessary.

Use when needed for garnish.

Reserve the oil that is now infused with shallot flavor for preparing any kind of Malaysian food.

MAKES 1 CUP.

NOTE   Follow the same instructions to prepare Crisp Fried Garlic Chips.

1   cup *cloves garlic*
1   cup corn oil for *deep frying*

Peel and slice the garlic into thin rounds. Fry over low heat for several minutes until the garlic turns brown. Remove with a slotted spoon to drain on paper towels.

Reserve the oil, which has a fine aromatic aroma and flavor, for cooking and/or salad dressing.

MAKES 1 CUP.

How to Make Tamarind Liquid

The beautiful tropical tamarind tree produces a seed pod filled with a black sticky pulp and black seeds the size of lima beans. This pulp has an attractive acid flavor and is used throughout the tropical world, including Latin America. The Malaysians sometimes refer to the liquid prepared from the tamarind paste as tamarind juice. The paste can be purchased in Chinatowns or East Indian shops in the United States.

¹/₄ *cup tamarind paste*
³/₄ *cup water*

1. Put the paste in a bowl, cover with the water, and let steep for ¹/₂ hour. Move the mixture around with your fingers now and then since it contains fibers and seeds.
2. Strain the mixture through a metal sieve and discard the impurities.

    The remaining liquid is used in Malaysia in curries, satays, and other traditional dishes.

MAKES ABOUT ³/₄ CUP.

How to Make Chili Boh (Chili Paste)

Chili boh is often used as a seasoning in cooking, as it is in Penang. It can also be served as a side dish, a hot chili paste, for those with incendiary palates.

It should be pointed out that chilis, fresh or dried, green or red, are not all created equal. They can be mildly or fiercely hot, and once you are aware of this difference then personal preference will influence the amount needed. The proof of the pudding is in the eating.

10 *fresh hot red chilis, or 10 hot red dried chilis*
 3 *tablespoons water*
¹/₂ *teaspoon salt*
 1 *tablespoon vegetable oil*

1. Process the fresh chilis into a paste with the 3 tablespoons of water or more and the salt. Should you prefer to use the dried chilis they must be broken up and steeped in water to cover for 15 minutes. Then drain and process with the salt into a paste.
2. Sauté the paste in the oil over low heat for 2 minutes. The *chili boh* is now ready for kitchen or table use.

    Store in a jar with a tight cover in the refrigerator.

MAKES ABOUT ¹/₃ CUP.

How to Make "Superior" Soup (Chinese of Ipoh)

This is the the traditional recipe of an Ipoh hawker family that has been handed down for five generations, from the great great grandfather to the present-day young man. This rich and intense soup can be used in any number of Chinese dishes where broth or stock is required. It is a good thing to have around and can be refrigerated for 5 days. Perhaps one half a recipe will be enough for the occasional homecooking of Malaysian dishes.

6	*pounds of chicken backs and bones*
1/2	*pound pork bones*
1	*fowl (4 pounds), cut into about 10 pieces*
1	*tablespoon dried soy beans*
1	*tablespoon black peppercorns*
2	*tablespoons sugar*
1	*tablespoon rock sugar (available in Chinese food stores)*
1	*tablespoon salt*
12	*quarts water*

Put everything in a very large pot and bring to a boil. Skim off the foam that rises, then simmer over low heat for 2 hours. Strain the soup and discard the bones and fowl.

During the cooking, about 2 quarts of water will evaporate. Refrigerate when not using.

MAKES ABOUT 9 QUARTS.

HOW TO MAKE KEROPOK (MALAY)

Keropok are those crisp crackers prepared from fish, shrimp, squid, and perhaps other seafood. In Indonesia, they are known as *krupuk*. The technique of making them is the same for all *keropok* and is a labor-intensive activity. Terengganu state on the east coast of Malaysia is a center of *keropok* manufacturing in small workshops. Here is how it was done in one shop.

1. Sardines are cut into fillets and mixed with sago flour in equal proportions. Salt and enough water is added to make a moist, firm combination, which is then processed to a more or less smooth paste.
2. The mixture is then rolled by hand into sausage rolls 6 to 8 inches long and ½ inch in diameter.
3. The fresh *keropok* rolls can be boiled or fried and eaten out of hand as a snack for breakfast with chili sauce dip.
4. For purposes of drying and preserving (the state that *keropok* are normally found in shops), the rolls are boiled and set aside for 2 days. They are then sliced thin and dried in the sun until they are quite hard. Then they are ready to be sold.
5. To reconstitute *keropok* for snacks or as an adjunct to a meal, the dried slices are deep fried in hot oil for a matter of seconds, at which time they expand rapidly, curling into crisp shapes. I always drain them on paper towels to remove excess oil.

Dried *keropok* in various flavors can be purchased in Southeast Asian, Malaysian, Thai, and Indonesian food shops.

HOW TO MAKE SAMBAL POWDER

1/2   *cup yellow split peas*
1/2   *cup* chana ka dal *(yellow split lentils)*
1 1/4   *cups coriander seed*
1   *tablespoon fenugreek seed*
3   *ounces hot red dried chilis, or less, to taste*

1. In a skillet or wok dry roast each ingredient individually until the aroma arises. Let them cool.
2. Combine all the roasted ingredients and grind to a powder in a spice grinder or mortar and pestle.

    Store in a jar with a tight cover at room temperature.

MAKES ABOUT 3/4 CUP POWDER.

How to Make Kurma Powder

This is the Malay-Indian style of preparing *kurma* powder, which is to say in the same way that curry powders are prepared. One may also use prepared *kurma* powder, as so many do now in Malaysia and elsewhere.

There is no hot red dried chili in this preparation, which would give the powder a red color.

3   *tablespoons coriander seed*
2   *tablespoons black peppercorns*
2½   *tablespoons fennel seed*
2   *tablespoons cumin seed*
2   *tablespoons roasted cashew nuts*

Grind all the ingredients together into a fine powder.
Store in a jar with a tight cover at room temperature.

MAKES ABOUT ³/₄ CUP.

How to Make Malaysian Garam Masala

Garam masala means "hot mixed spices" and is so commonly used in Indian cooking that it is always referred to by its Hindi name.

Spices lose their strength and influence in a dish when they are old or are not stored well. Spices should always be stored in a container (I prefer a glass jar) with a tight cover. Also, prepare or purchase spices in small quantities and use them up before purchasing more. In this way, you will always have a supply of fresh spices that retain their natural essences.

2	*tablespoons coriander seed*
1	*tablespoon cumin seed*
1	*tablespoon cardamom pods*
	a 1-inch piece cinnamon stick
1	*tablespoon black peppercorns*
1	*teaspoon whole cloves (4)*
1/4	*teaspoon ground nutmeg*

Toast the spices lightly in a nonstick skillet over low heat for about 1 minute, or until the aroma rises. Grind the spices together in a food processor to a fine powder. Store in a glass jar with a tight cover.

MAKES ABOUT 1/4 CUP.

NOTE Garam masala varies according to regional tastes and personal preference. The above recipe is from the Terengganu district on mainland Malaysia.

How to Make Lihing (Sticky Rice Wine)

I first tasted sticky rice wine in an ethnic tribal community (Kadazan) in Sabah and was immediately converted to the taste. The wine is lightly murky, with an attractive sweetness that is enticing. The drink is traditional at weddings and other celebrations.

The yeast for making the wine was available in the central market and consisted of miniature white doughnut shapes, 1¼ inches in diameter and about ½ inch thick. Known as sweet yeast balls, they were sold tied together in a large necklace. One purchased as many as needed.

2   *cups glutinous (also called "sticky") rice*
2   *yeast rings, ground to a fine powder*

1. Boil the rice in water for about 20 minutes, until tender enough to be eaten. Drain excess liquid and cool well. Spread the rice out to cool on a baking sheet.
2. Scatter the powdered yeast over the rice and mix it in thoroughly. Then put the rice in a clay or glass jar, cover, and allow to ferment at room temperature, preferably in the kitchen, where there is some warmth.

    The rice should be allowed to ferment from 1 week to 1 month, the longer the better, before wine accumulates and can be drunk or used in Manuk Lihing (Chicken in Rice Wine, page 75).

MAKES ABOUT 1 QUART.

INDEX